Streamlining Non-Tariff Measures

Streamlining Non-Tariff Measures

A Toolkit for Policy Makers

Olivier Cadot, Mariem Malouche, and Sebastián Sáez

THE WORLD BANK
Washington, D.C.

ISBN (paper): 978-0-8213-9510-3
ISBN (electronic): 978-0-8213-9511-0
DOI: 10.1596/978-0-8213-9510-3

Library of Congress Cataloging-in-Publication Data
Cadot, Olivier.
    Streamlining non-tariff measures : a toolkit for policymakers / Olivier Cadot, Mariem Malouche, and Sebastián Sáez.
        p. cm.
    Includes bibliographical references and index.
    ISBN 978-0-8213-9510-3 -- ISBN 978-0-8213-9511-0 (electronic)
1. Non-tariff trade barriers. 2. Foreign trade regulation. 3. Commercial policy. I. Malouche, Mariem, 1973- II. Sáez, Sebastián. III. World Bank. IV. Title.
    HF1430.C34 2012
    382'.5--dc23

                                                                          2012010813

Cover photo: Pete Gardner

Contents

Foreword   *ix*
Acknowledgments   *xiii*
About the Authors   *xv*
Abbreviations   *xvii*

	Overview	1
Chapter 1	**NTMs: Definition, Data, and International Regulations**	9
	The New NTM Dataset	10
	Living Up to International Commitments	21
	Notes	33
	References	34
Chapter 2	**Streamlining NTMs: The Issues**	37
	Beginning the NTM Review	40
	Reassessing the Benefits of Government Intervention	41
	Reassessing the Costs of Government Intervention	46
	Assessing the Sourcing Costs of NTMs	48

	Balancing Costs and Benefits	52
	Notes	59
	References	60

Chapter 3   **Streamlining NTMs: Processes and Institutions**   **63**
Getting the Institutional Setup Right   64
Steps in the NTM Review Process   72
Annex: Approaches to Streamlining Existing
NTMs   81
Notes   83
References   84

Chapter 4   **Country and Region Experiences with**
Streamlining NTMs   **87**
Unilaterally Driven Reforms   87
Reforms Anchored in Regional Integration   108
Notes   118
References   119

Chapter 5   **Streamlining NTMs: Case Studies**   **121**
An SPS Measure: Import Ban and Environmental
Protection   121
A TBT Measure and Incoherence along the
Value Chain   127
Prohibition and Its Impact on Welfare   128
Notes   132

Appendix A   **UNCTAD NTM Classification,**
February 2012   **133**

Appendix B   **Request Form for NTM Review**   **171**

Appendix C   **Questionnaire for the Review of Existing NTMs**   **173**

Appendix D   **Price Gap and Welfare**   **179**

Boxes
2.1   NTMs and the Case for Risk Management in
Border Agencies   58
3.1   Brazil Challenges in Regulatory Reforms:
Some Preliminary Lessons   65

3.2   Institutional Setup to Streamline New NTMs
       in Indonesia   70
3.3   Regulatory Reform in Mexico   74
4.1   Mexico Standards Modernization: The Case of
       Food Labeling   94
4.2   Two Regulations That Hurt the Competitiveness of
       Mauritian Firms   99
4.3   The Tripartite NTB Monitoring Mechanism   114
4.4   CEFTA and TBTs   117
5.1   Risks to the Environment: A Biologist's Expert Opinion   125

Figures

O.1   NTM Toolkit Flowchart   5
1.1   NTM Classification by Chapter (first tier)   11
1.2   Frequency Index and Coverage Ratios by Chapter
       of NTM   13
1.3   Frequency Index and Coverage Ratios by Region and
       Chapter of NTM   15
1.4   Frequency Indices and Coverage Ratios, by Country   16
1.5   Seven Most Prevailing Types of NTMs Experienced by
       Surveyed Companies as NTBs, by Regional Destination   20
2.1   Flowchart of an NTM Review   42
2.2   Costs and Benefits of a Technical Regulation: The Case of
       Organic Shrimp   54
3.1   Political Commitment and NTM Reforms   64
3.2   Sample Institutional Setup for NTM Review   69
3.3   SOPs for Introducing NTMs in the Indonesia Ministry
       of Trade   71
3.4   Review Process Flow   76
4.1   Numbers of Products Subject to NTMs in Indonesia   104
4.2   NTMs Issued by Agency   105
5.1   Decline in Mauritius Exports of Cut Flowers
       (HS 060310)   123
5.2   Real-Income Gain from Eliminating Import
       Bans, by Income Level and Product Category   131

Tables

1.1   NTMs Experienced by Exporting Companies as NTBs   19
2.1   BCC Categories of Compliance Costs   47
2.2   Average Domestic Price Indices by Category
       (world average = 100), Indonesia and the Philippines   51

4.1   NTM Classification Following WTO Consistency
         Criteria   110
B4.3.1   NTBs Cited in the NTBMM   115
5.1   Nigeria's Prohibited Imports   129
5.2   Price Gap Calculations, Lagos vs. Nairobi
         (% of price gap)   130

Foreword

As discussed in depth in the World Trade Organization's (WTO) 2012 World Trade Report, *Beyond Tariffs: NTMs and Services Measures in the 21st Century,* the trade policy landscape has changed. Indirect policies are increasingly replacing tariffs to hinder free trade between countries. Recent World Bank analysis based on World Trade Organization (WTO) monitoring reports and data from the Global Trade Alert (a network of think tanks around the globe) shows that the number of non-tariff measures (NTMs)—including quotas, import licensing requirements, and discriminatory government procurement rules—increased in the first two years post-2008, and rose sharply in 2011. India, China, Indonesia, Argentina, the Russian Federation, and Brazil together accounted for almost half of all the new NTMs imposed worldwide. Although many NTMs are justified on the basis of health or safety standards, they can also be used to act as barriers to trade and are put in place for protectionist purposes.

More governments across World Bank clients are requesting help in removing non-tariff *barriers* and improving their trade competitiveness. The International Trade Department has developed this toolkit to assist stakeholders in better assessing and streamlining NTMs. The first step is data collection, which is essential in understanding and quantifying the impact of NTMs on trade. The World Bank has been an active participant in international efforts to improve data collection on NTMs, including as a member of the Multi-Agency Support Team (MAST) of Eminent Experts led by the United Nations Conference on Trade and Development (UNCTAD). The World Bank is a partner—along with the International Trade Centre, UNCTAD, and the African Development Bank—in the recently launched Transparency in Trade initiative. One objective of this initiative is to join forces in collecting data on NTMs. As of April 2012, NTM data have been collected in about 30 developing countries. Efforts are also being made to increase the local capacity of governments and think tanks to maintain live databases and analyze the impact of NTMs.

The essence of *Streamlining Non-Tariff Measures: A Toolkit for Policy Makers* is to help policy makers and analysts navigate through the maze of issues to consider when engaged in trade competitiveness and business regulatory improvement agendas. It offers a novel approach to addressing NTMs by recognizing the complexity and variety of NTMs in terms of their objectives, policy measures, procedures, and economic and societal impact. The toolkit introduces the reader to analytical approaches to assessing economic costs and benefits that can be applied, depending on the measure and the capacity of governments. It also provides a framework for helping governments build an adequate institutional setup to address NTMs as a cross-cutting issue involving several government agencies and stakeholders. The toolkit is practical and includes questionnaires and guidelines to better evaluate the underlying issues that existing NTMs are trying to address, and to devise recommendations. It also walks the reader through country and regional experiences with tackling the NTM agenda.

Streamlining Non-Tariff Measures: A Toolkit for Policy Makers aims to shift policy makers' and economists' mindsets on how to address NTMs, the new frontier in trade policy. NTMs may be legitimate measures addressing market or coordination failures and achieving a wide range of policy objectives, from consumers' safety and health to environment purposes. However, when poorly designed, they can hurt competitiveness and unnecessarily raise the cost of living. Restricted access to key inputs and intermediate products, and cumbersome procedures for import and export licenses and permits cause delays and extra costs to firms, hurting small and medium enterprises particularly and dampening diversification efforts. NTMs can also increase the cost of important food staples and household consumer products, putting more pressure on the poorest. While some non-tariff measures evidently do not intend to restrict trade, they are considered non-tariff barriers (NTBs) when they are overly trade restrictive. The challenge is to identify ways to reduce the trade-impeding effect of NTMs while ensuring that legitimate regulatory objectives are attained. The objective of eliminating NTMs without a comprehensive analysis is often doomed because it does not take into account their multi-purpose nature.

We expect this toolkit to help governments and donors find win-win solutions to trade-regulation issues and to contribute to an agenda of regulatory governance in a large number of countries.

Mona Haddad
Sector Manager
International Trade Department

Acknowledgments

This volume was written by Mariem Malouche (Task Team Leader), Olivier Cadot, and Sebastián Sáez. The authors are grateful to Ndiame Diop and Gaël Raballand for their comments on the toolkit and to Enrique Aldaz-Caroll and Ian Gillson for their comments on the concept note circulated at the early stages of the project. Thanks are also extended to World Bank International Trade Department colleagues who provided helpful feedback at an internal seminar, as well as to Scott Jacobs from Jacobs and Associates who commented on chapter 3. The team has also benefited greatly from their involvement with the country teams of Mauritius and Indonesia and would like to extend special thanks to Sawkut Rojid (Mauritius) and Sjamsu Rahardja (Indonesia) for their invaluable input. Thanks also to Rebecca Martin for patiently formatting the toolkit and to Charumathi Rao for her administrative support. The book was produced under the overall supervision of Mona Haddad (Sector Manager) and Bernard Hoekman (Sector Director) in the International Trade Department of the World Bank. Last but not least, the authors thank the governments of Finland, Norway, Sweden, and the United Kingdom for their financial support under the Multi-Donor Trust Fund for Trade and Development.

About the Authors

Olivier Cadot is professor of International Economics and director of the Institute of Applied Economics at the University of Lausanne, Switzerland. Before that, he was associate professor of economics at INSEAD (European Institute of Business Administration). He has held visiting appointments at the University of California at Los Angeles and McGill University (Montreal), New York University, Université d'Auvergne (France), Koç University (Istanbul), the Paris School of Economics, and the Institut d'Études Politiques de Paris. He was a senior economist in the World Bank Trade Department between 2009 and 2011 and has advised the French government, the Swiss federal government, and the European Commission on trade policy matters. He also worked for the Organisation for Economic Co-operation and Development and the International Monetary Fund. He was elected best teacher of the year at HEC (Hautes Etudes Commerciales) Lausanne and was nominated three times for the outstanding teacher award at INSEAD. He has contributed regularly to international executive programs. He is a research fellow of the Center for Economic Policy Research in London, a senior fellow of the FERDI (Fondation pour les Etudes et Recherches sur le Développement International) and associate scholar at CEPREMAP (Center for Economic Research and Its Applications). He also serves on the editorial board of the *Revue d'Économie du Développement* and on the scientific advisory board of the Fondation Jean-Monnet pour l'Europe. He has published numerous scholarly papers on international trade and economic development. Cadot holds a PhD in economics from Princeton University and a master's degree in economic history from McGill University.

Mariem Malouche is an economist in the World Bank International Trade Department within the Poverty Reduction and Economic Management Network. She joined the World Bank in 2004 as an economist in the Middle East and North Africa Region. Before joining the Bank, Malouche earned a PhD in international economics from Université Paris-Dauphine, France. Her areas of interest include trade policy, non-tariff measures, regional integration, export diversification, and trade finance. She also has experience in the South Asia and Africa Regions. She is co-editor of *Trade Finance during the Great Trade Collapse* (World Bank 2011).

Sebastián Sáez is a senior trade economist at the World Bank International Trade Department. After studying economics at the University of Chile, he earned a master's degree in public sector economics at the Catholic University of Rio de Janeiro, Brazil. His areas of expertise are trade policy, trade in services, and WTO (World Trade Organization) trade law and regional trade agreements. He has published articles on international economic relations and the book *Estrategia y Negociación en el Sistema Multilateral de Comercio*, Dolmen Ediciones (1999). He is also coeditor of a number of World Bank books: *International Trade in Services: New Trends and Opportunities for Developing Countries* (2010), *Exporting Services: A Developing Country Perspective* (2012), and *Trade in Services Negotiations: A Guide for Developing Countries* (2010).

Abbreviations

ALADI	*Asociación Latino-Americana de Integración* (Latin American Integration Association)
ALOP	appropriate level of protection
ASEAN	Association of Southeast Asian Nations
AVE	ad-valorem equivalent
CDE	Economic Deregulation Council (Mexico)
CEFTA	Central European Free Trade Agreement
COCEX	*Comisión de Comercio Exterior,* International Trade Commission (Mexico)
COFEMER	Comisión Federal de Mejora Regulatoria (Mexico)
COFEPRIS	*Comisión Federal para la Protección contra Riesgos Sanitarios,* Federal Commission for the Protection Against Sanitary Risks (Mexico)
COL	cost-of-living
COMESA	Common Market for Eastern and Southern Africa
DID	difference in differences
EAC	East African Community
EIU	Economist Intelligence Unit
EN	Euro Norm (European Standards)
EU	European Union

FAO	UN Food and Agriculture Organization
FTA	free trade agreement
GATT	General Agreement on Tariffs and Trade
GDP	gross domestic product
GMO	genetically modified organisms
HS	Harmonized System
ICP	World Bank International Comparison Program
INSW	Indonesian National Single Window
ISO	International Organization for Standardization
ITC	International Trade Centre
LCE	Foreign Trade Law (Mexico)
MAST	Multi-Agency Support Team
MENA	Middle East and North Africa Region
MFN	most favored nation
MSB	Mauritius Standards Bureau
NAFTA	North American Free Trade Agreement
NGO	non-governmental organization
NOMs	mandatory technical rules (Mexico)
NPIK	Specific Importer Identification Number (Indonesia)
NPV	net present value
NTB	non-tariff barrier
NTBMM	NTB Monitoring Mechanism (SADC)
NTM	non-tariff measure
OECD	Organisation for Economic Co-operation and Development
PRC	Permit Review Committee (Mauritius)
PSI	pre-shipment inspection
QALY	quality-adjusted life years
QR	quantitative restriction
RIA	regulatory impact assessment
SACU	Southern African Customs Union
SADC	Southern African Development Community
SCM	Standard Cost Model
SME	small and medium enterprises
SOP	standard operating procedure
SPS	sanitary and phytosanitary
TBT	technical barriers to trade
TRAINS	TRade Analysis and INformation System
TRQ	tariff-rate quota

UDE	Economic Deregulation Unit (Mexico)
UN	United Nations
UNCTAD	UN Conference on Trade and Development
UNIDO	UN Industrial Development Organization
WHO	World Health Organization
WTO	World Trade Organization
WTP	willingness to pay

Overview

This volume aims to assist policy makers in reviewing and improving "non-tariff measures" (NTMs), that is, policies other than tariffs that affect international trade. Traditionally, NTMs have been perceived and defined solely as non-tariff *barriers* (NTBs) that governments needed to remove in order to facilitate trade. This toolkit provides a new, practical approach to designing NTMs that carefully balances the reduction of trade costs against the preservation of public objectives. It is also intended to encourage governments to address the NTM agenda from domestic competitiveness and poverty perspectives, rather than from a mercantilist standpoint of concessions to trading partners. The basic question to be addressed is neatly summarized by the World Trade Organization (WTO), with regard to sanitary and phytosanitary (SPS) measures:

> How do you ensure that your country's consumers are being supplied with food that is safe to eat—"safe" by the standards you consider appropriate? And at the same time, how can you ensure that strict health and safety regulations are not being used as an excuse for protecting domestic producers? (WTO 2012).

Defining and Classifying NTMs

Addressing the NTM issue has become prominent in the policy agendas of governments seeking to further integrate their trade into the world economy. As the overall level of tariff protection has been largely contained around the world through multilateral, regional, and unilateral tariff reductions, streamlining NTMs—whether quantitative restrictions, technical regulations, or anticompetitive measures, to name but a few—is nowadays one of the new frontiers of trade policy.

Non-tariff measures can also be hijacked as protectionist tools or as weapons in trade wars. In a recent incident, China announced a ban on imports of Argentine soya oil worth US$2 billion, stating that Argentine oil failed to meet China's quality standards—but it also acknowledged that the move was a reprisal for Argentine anti-dumping measures in textile and other sectors (*Financial Times*, April 5, 2010).

Firm surveys on the impact of NTMs, like those conducted by the International Trade Centre, have repeatedly shown that, even without protectionist intent, NTMs can raise trade costs, divert managerial attention, and penalize small exporters and those located in low-income countries where access to legal and regulatory information is difficult. Countries imposing NTMs may end up hurting their own competitiveness by making it difficult for domestic producers and exporters to access critical inputs in a timely fashion.

For all their potentially trade-restricting effects, however, NTMs should not be thought of as merely what their name suggests—a trade-policy instrument like a tariff but in a different legal form. They are fundamentally different from tariffs in a number of ways. First, there are different types of NTMs. In the new classification adopted by the United Nations Conference on Trade and Development, the term covers measures as different as quotas, technical regulations, SPS measures, preshipment inspection, and forced channels. In addition, the motivation and effects of these measures are very different, as are the tools needed to understand them. Moreover, the composition of NTMs has been rapidly evolving. Quantitative restrictions (for example, quotas and non-automatic licensing), which clearly are trade-policy instruments, are on the decline, whereas technical regulations (product standards and SPS measures on agri-food products), often not primarily trade motivated, are on the rise.

Technical regulations respond to a public demand for traceability and protection against health and environmental hazards. This demand, which is highest in Organisation for Economic Co-operation and Development (OECD) countries, can be expected to grow everywhere in the world, including in developing countries, as income levels rise and media attention gives high salience to food, health, and environmental crises. The fundamental implication is that the prevalence of NTMs should be expected to increase not shrink, reflecting the response of governments to a universal societal demand for public goods.

The thinking on NTMs has not kept pace with their changing reality for several reasons. First, for many years, research on NTMs has suffered from a lack of transparency. Until recently, only one year of data (2001) was available for a sufficiently wide set of countries through the TRAINS (TRade Analysis and INformation System) database, severely hampering analysis. This situation is being remedied through a multi-agency joint venture to collect a new wave of NTM data and put in place structures for sustainable data collection and publication. The objective of the data collection effort is to encourage every country, through dialogue and technical assistance, to publish and maintain an up-to-date inventory of all non-tariff measures in force, and to guarantee its accuracy at all times.

A second problem is that the methods used to analyze NTMs are largely derived from traditional trade-policy analysis, which may provide only a partial angle on their effects. One of the most popular methods to measure the incidence of NTMs consists of calculating the proportion of products covered by one or more NTMs (the so-called "frequency ratio") or the proportion of trade value (the "coverage ratio"). The problem with relying on such ratios to measure progress in NTM streamlining is that it inevitably leads to setting targets in terms of removal of NTMs, which is of limited usefulness, given rising demands for regulation for safety and consumer protection.

A more sophisticated approach intended to measure the *severity* of NTMs' effects, was devised by Hiao Looi Kee, Alessandro Nicita, and Marcelo Olarreaga (2009) at the World Bank. The method is to estimate ad-valorem equivalents (AVEs) of NTMs[1] through cross-country econometrics. This method provides useful information on the trade restricting effect of NTMs. However, it can be only a first step in policy dialogue. Suppose that a ban on the import of a certain agricultural product is deemed necessary by scientists to protect local biodiversity, but that the ban raises the domestic price of the product in question by a very high AVE. Should the ban be lifted? Clearly, the AVE alone provides only half the story.

Slow Progress in Policy Development

The inappropriate definition of NTMs, by considering them solely as trade barriers and not recognizing their other often legitimate policy objectives, has contributed to the slow progress in policy dialogue and in negotiations at both multilateral and regional levels. The disappointing results are particularly striking at the regional level, where NTM streamlining and harmonization have been high on the agenda of regional secretariats for years without much action on the ground. The Association of Southeast Asian Nations (ASEAN) provides an interesting example of progress at the sectoral level, with a mutual recognition agreement on cosmetics largely resulting from a strong push by industry leaders. While private-sector involvement in NTM streamlining is key to its progress, large multinational corporations are unlikely to have much stake in local public goods. Thus, relying exclusively on industry lobbying to drive the process may lead to an unbalanced approach where private-sector market access has primacy over local public goods, irrespective of costs and benefits.

Trade economists and lawyers have tried to get around the conceptual definition of NTMs by drawing a distinction between non-tariff *measures* (NTMs) and non-tariff *barriers* (NTBs). The latter are the "evil" form of the former, wherein trade restrictiveness, whether or not deliberate, exceeds what is needed for the measure's non-trade objectives. Conceptually, the various types of NTMs could be categorized as either NTMs or NTBs, and given color codes—green, amber, or red—as in agricultural negotiations. However, such an approach is unlikely to result in progress, because what matters on the ground typically has more to do with *how* measures are applied than *what* measures are applied. For instance, a technical standard may create unnecessary problems because it requires certification of foreign production facilities. Or an SPS measure may be highly trade-inhibiting because it requires every shipment to be inspected, rather than using risk profiling and reducing the number of inspections.

In other words, the devil is in the details. This toolkit is predicated on the idea that the complexity and diversity of NTMs should be recognized, and that the process of streamlining them should start from there. Problems should be identified at the country level through consultations with the private sector, and technical solutions should be sought through careful analysis and private/public dialogue. The underlying philosophy is similar to what is known as "regulatory improvement" or "regulatory impact assessment" (RIA) (figure O.1). However, where RIA is used to analyze measures before they are adopted, this toolkit is designed for the review of existing measures as a response to specific demands from countries struggling with legacies of complicated and penalizing regulations. Dealing with existing measures has the advantage of responding to an immediate need and focusing on measures whose effects are known. However, the regulatory improvement of existing NTMs should be thought of as only the first stage of a process of regulatory improvement also covering the flow of new ones, to prevent having to start streamlining efforts all over again when poorly designed new measures keep on appearing.

The toolkit proposes that governments put in place adequate structures to make streamlining NTMs an owned and sustained effort. Technical assistance on regulatory improvements, whether by development agencies or consulting firms, has tended to focus on "quick wins," useful to gather short-term political support and momentum. A more sustainable institutional setup would ensure continuity in the process of improving the trade competitiveness of firms as the business environment evolves and the stock of regulations grows. The process of regulatory improvement should

Figure O.1   NTM Toolkit Flowchart

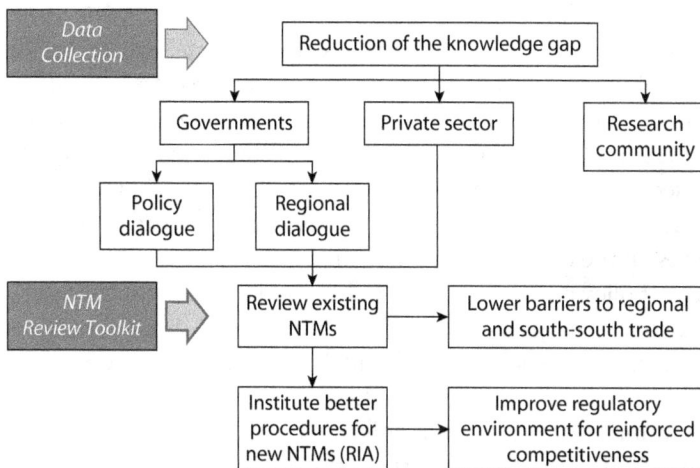

Note: NTM = non-tariff measure, RIA = regulatory impact assessment.

be based on three pillars—dialogue, analysis, and broad participation—by instituting the following:

- A body dedicated to public-private dialogue (for example, an NTM committee) serving as an entry point for the private sector to flag problems and contribute to the solution.
- A technical team dedicated to carrying out substantial analysis (for example, a permanent secretariat for the NTM committee) with analytical capabilities akin to those of a productivity or competition commission, to lead the dialogue into policy action.
- Outside expertise and collaboration by drawing into the review process line ministries involved in the issuance and enforcement of NTMs to ensure broad participation and ownership.

This basic structure can be adapted to various country situations in terms of location of the effort (which ministry), degree of independence, and so on. Its primary strength is that it creates a sound basis for the transformation of a review process for existing measures into a quality-control system for new ones.

This toolkit also supports more robust analytics adjusted to local capabilities. The "RIA industry" has responded to the problem of limited analytical capabilities in developing countries by reducing the complexity of the process. Simplification from full-fledged cost-benefit analysis in most cases is inevitable—even desirable. However, box-checking approaches may miss subtle but important design or implementation issues that only detailed case studies can uncover.

The toolkit is based on the idea that, with adequate technical assistance and use of local resources—universities and think tanks—sufficiently detailed analysis can be carried out, but that the *form* of the review setup should be adjusted to local capabilities. For instance, when the NTM committee secretariat does not have sufficient internal capabilities, it may act simply as a hub to coordinate analytical input from outside and inside the ministries. In the case of some NTMs that aim at addressing non-trade yet legitimate policy objectives, only a full-fledged cost-benefit analysis would help all concerned parties (both lines ministries and the private sector) reach a consensus, such as an alternative, less trade-restrictive measure that achieves the same policy objective.

This volume is organized as follows. Chapter 1 discusses the newly revamped NTM classification system, the data collection effort so far, and the key characteristics of the data. It also highlights the private-sector view that NTMs should support domestic firms' competitiveness across countries. In addition, it reviews WTO and OECD guidelines for designing trade regulations, and presents the regional dimension of addressing standards and technical barriers to trade.

Chapter 2 describes the analytics of an NTM review, step by step through the key questions—for example, is there a market failure, which market is affected, what are the costs of regulatory action vs. the risks of deregulation—and explains how to answer these questions and how to go about quantification when it is possible. The chapter emphasizes a balanced approach to NTM review, covering both the evaluation of trade and administrative costs and the conceptual and quantitative evaluation of non-trade regulatory benefits.

Chapter 3 focuses on the institutional setup and key principles required to successfully pursue the streamlining of regulations. Since the mid-1990s, developed countries have introduced new regulatory approaches aimed at improving the quality of the decision-making process by enhancing both the analytical framework used by policy makers and the participation of interested parties in the regulatory process. Although proposed instruments, such as regulatory impact assessments, have been widely incorporated in a number of developed and developing countries, countries have followed different institutional settings to implement them into their legal systems. In some cases, a centralized approach has been followed, whereby a central authority is responsible for overseeing the implementation of best regulatory practices, while in other cases a more decentralized approach shared among ministries is followed with the idea that it favors the adoption of best practices by all relevant ministries.

Finally, chapters 4 and 5 provide practical examples of streamlining NTMs. Chapter 4 overviews selected experiences with tackling the trade regulatory agenda at both country and regional levels. On one hand, the examples of Mexico in North America and Mauritius in Africa illustrate how these economies arrived at a regulatory-improvement agenda intended to reinforce the competitiveness of domestic firms and overcome financial crises. Mexico's experience in the 1990s shows that regulatory reform (of which NTM streamlining is part) was demanded by *domestic* private operators as a way of reducing the cost of doing business domestically and across borders. On the other hand, the examples of Indonesia and other countries in Eastern Europe and Africa illustrate the opportunities regional agreements offer to anchor regulatory reforms. Chapter 5 presents case studies on streamlining NTMs, including technical regulation and prohibition, particularly illustrating the analytics that may support the review process.

Note that this toolkit should not be viewed as a stand-alone product, but as part of a suite of integrated knowledge products offered by the World Bank International Trade Department, including a competitiveness toolkit and a trade facilitation toolkit (Reis and Farole 2012; World Bank 2010). Sometimes NTMs create barriers to trade because of the way border-management agencies enforce them. In such cases, NTM reviews naturally lead to trade-facilitation reviews, and the two products (NTM-review and trade-facilitation toolkits) should be used together.

Finally, NTM reviews should be seen as part of national competitiveness agendas rather than as concessions to trading partners. When NTMs are perceived by the domestic private sector as hampering access to key inputs, business regulatory reviews should naturally lead to NTM reviews. Joint use of the triangle of products will facilitate the adoption by governments of coherent national competitiveness strategies centered around the reduction of trade costs.

Note

1. The ad-valorem equivalent of an NTM is the rate of a (hypothetical) tariff that would generate an equivalent reduction in imports.

References

Financial Times. 2010. "Argentine Soya Rift with China Grows." April 5.

Kee, Hiau Looi, Alessandro Nicita, and Marcelo Olarreaga. 2009. "Estimating Trade Restrictiveness Indices." *Economic Journal* 119 (534): 172–99.

Reis, Jose Guilherme, and Thomas Farole. 2012. "Trade Competitiveness Diagnostic Toolkit." Trade and Development, World Bank, Washington, DC.

World Bank. 2010. "Trade and Transport Facilitation Assessment: A Practical Toolkit for Country Implementation." World Bank Study, World Bank, Washington, DC. http://siteresources.worldbank.org/EXTTLF/Resources/Trade&Transport_Facilitation_Assessment_Practical_Toolkit.pdf.

WTO (World Trade Organization). 2012. "WTO Trade Topics: Sanitary and Phytosanitary Measures." http://www.wto.org/english/tratop_e/tratop_e.htm.

CHAPTER 1

NTMs: Definition, Data, and International Regulations

Efforts to streamline NTMs have been hampered by lack of a clear conceptual definition and data on the use of NTMs, their impact on domestic competitiveness, and their implications for market access for developing countries. Most studies on the impact of NTMs still rely on obsolete or fragmentary data. Part of the reason for this lack of visibility is that collecting data on NTMs is a difficult endeavor. Unlike tariffs, NTMs are not mere numbers—they are complex legal texts that are not easily amenable to quantification, comparison, or even standard formatting. The difficulty in collecting and analyzing information on NTMs was highlighted by the recent two-year activities of the Multi-Agency Support Team (MAST)[1] convened by the Secretary-General of the United Nations Conference on Trade and Development (UNCTAD) and its Group of Eminent Persons on NTBs (GNTB).

This chapter presents the result of the MAST activities on NTM data on three fronts: the revamped NTM classification, new data collection initiatives, and firm survey results on the impact of NTMs on the business sector (MAST 2009; UNCTAD 2010). Finally, the chapter concludes with an overview of the two most important international guiding principles for designing NTMs: the WTO and OECD guidelines.

The New NTM Dataset

Given the broad definition of NTMs and the lack of comparable, up-to-date data, the international community has launched a major effort to gather and make available data on NTMs across countries. UNCTAD established the MAST, which led the data collection and revision of NTM classification. The MAST first established a common definition for NTMs: "policy measures, other than ordinary customs tariffs, that can potentially have an economic effect on international trade in goods, changing quantities traded, or prices, or both" (MAST 2009). Thus, an NTM is a measure that generates a wedge between the domestic and world prices of one or several traded goods or services.

The new MAST classification of NTMs, adopted in 2010, follows a hierarchical "tree" structure where NTMs are differentiated according to 16 branches, or chapters, denoted alphabetically, with three levels of sub-branches designated by one, two, and three-digit codes. This classification draws on the now outdated UNCTAD Coding System of Trade Control Measures classification of NTMs, which was modified and expanded by adding various categories of measures to reflect current trading conditions.

The classification includes many new subcategories of sanitary and phytosanitary (SPS) measures and technical barriers to trade (TBT), and introduces new NTM categories, including export measures, trade-related investment measures, distribution restrictions, restrictions on post-sales services, subsidies, measures related to intellectual property rights and rules of origin (figure 1.1). The classification also introduces the concept of "procedural obstacles," which refers to issues related to the process of application of an NTM, rather than the measure itself. There data are collected through surveys by the government agencies responsible for enforcing these procedures. The NTM classification has further been revised by UNCTAD after consultation with the World Trade Organization (WTO) in 2012. The latest version is provided in appendix A.

The MAST launched the collection of NTM data in seven pilot countries starting in 2008, which has helped refine the NTM classification and assess the pervasiveness of NTMs for the private sector (UNCTAD 2010). The World Bank has subsequently followed this effort by funding data collection in 16 developing countries, including 8 in Africa; 5 in the Middle East and North Africa; and 3 in East and South Asia. These initial efforts will be reinforced with a more long-standing effort led by the World Bank, International Trade Center (ITC), and UNCTAD to ensure sustainable funding resources for the collection of NTMs in most economies over the next five years as part of the Transparency in Trade initiative

Figure 1.1   NTM Classification by Chapter (first tier)

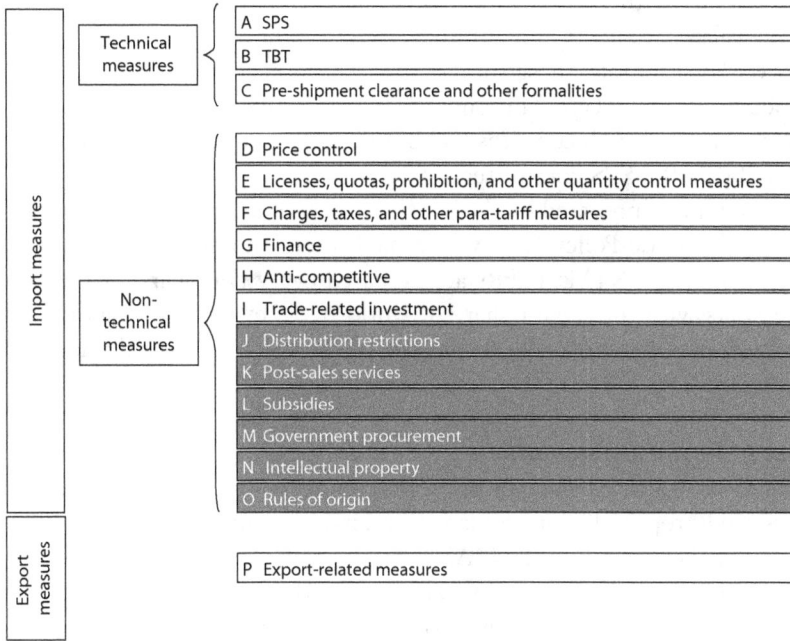

Import measures	Technical measures	A SPS
		B TBT
		C Pre-shipment clearance and other formalities
	Non-technical measures	D Price control
		E Licenses, quotas, prohibition, and other quantity control measures
		F Charges, taxes, and other para-tariff measures
		G Finance
		H Anti-competitive
		I Trade-related investment
		J Distribution restrictions
		K Post-sales services
		L Subsidies
		M Government procurement
		N Intellectual property
		O Rules of origin
Export measures		P Export-related measures

Source: MAST 2009.
Note: NTM data are collected only for categories A–I. The shaded categories J–P are used only to collect information from the private sector through surveys and web portals.

(http://www.tntdata.org/). Data collection will be conducted through local capacity-building so that the data are collected regularly to remain up to date.

This effort is a major improvement over the data available through the WTO notification system for SPS and TBT regulations, which has been unsatisfactory as a repository of information on all NTMs. WTO notification requirements have traditionally served diverse purposes, and the information they require from their members depends on the policy objective of the regulations. The SPS and TBT notification requirements, for example, aim to allow other members to influence the regulations that the member providing the notification plans to adopt. They do not require members to provide information on regulations that pre-dated the SPS and TBT Agreements, nor on the final form of the proposed new measures. Thus, the information collected through the WTO notification system provides only partial coverage, which may be insufficient from a transparency perspective (Bacchetta, Richtering, and Santana 2012). However, a number of other WTO sources of information on NTMs could be tapped into with a view to improving the transparency of trade data and trade-related policies and fulfilling some of the objectives mentioned above. For example, these sources include the records of discussions on "specific trade concerns" in some WTO committees. At the end of 2010, more than 270 such concerns had been discussed in the TBT committee and 290 in the SPS committee.

The reports prepared by the WTO Secretariat and the WTO members under the Trade Policy Review Mechanism are another major source of information on NTMs. (TPRs are prepared every two years for the four members with the largest share of world trade, every four years for the next 16 members by order of the size of their share of world trade, and every six years for the remaining members.)

Rise of Technical Regulations

The newly collected database of NTMs comprises 29 developing countries plus the European Union and Japan, and it covers measures from chapters A to I, and chapter P of the MAST classification. Analysis of the data collected thus far points to the prevalence of trade technical regulations and standards (TBT and SPS measures). TBT affect about 30 percent of products and trade values and SPS affect slightly less than 15 percent of trade (figure 1.2).

The prevalence of TBT and SPS reflects a major change in the world trade landscape over the past two decades (WTO 2012). First, tariffs have come down with their lock-in under the multilateral agenda and bilateral and regional preferential agreements, reducing their prevalence as trade policy measures. Second, trade grew rapidly in the 1990s and 2000s, which growth was driven by a mix of technological change and policy reforms. And developing countries account for a steadily increasing share of global trade: their volume of exports rose more than fourfold between 1990 and 2009. Therefore, governments are increasingly called upon to respond to a variety of concerns raised by members of society in many areas, including the environment, animal welfare, and food safety, and are urged to develop technical regulations.

However, the large incidence of SPS and TBT raises concerns for developing countries' exports, particularly those with higher value-added and those in new and dynamic sectors of international trade. These measures impose quality and safety standards that often exceed multilaterally accepted norms. The cost of compliance of SPS and TBT is also higher in low-income countries because infrastructure and export services are often

Figure 1.2   Frequency Index and Coverage Ratios by Chapter of NTM

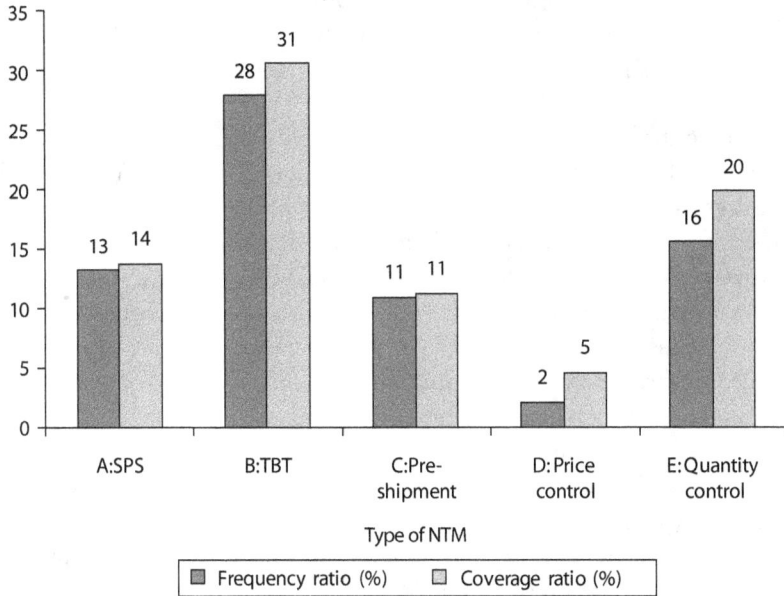

Source: Gourdon and Nicita 2012.

more expensive or must be outsourced abroad. SPS and TBT can practically erode the competitive advantage that developing countries have in lower labor costs and preferential access. Moreover, unlike prohibitions and quotas that are easily identifiable as "non-trade" NTBs, technical regulations may be adopted to achieve non-trade related legitimate domestic policy objectives. Responding to some of these concerns is a purely local or national matter, with little or no impact on trade or trade policy. But in the case of traded goods, these measures are becoming an increasingly important policy tool.

The second largest category of NTMs is quantity controls, which affect about 16 percent of products and 20 percent of trade. Only a small portion of these measures are still in the form of quotas and export restrictions, since most quantitative restrictions are illegal under WTO rules. Most of these measures are in the form of non-automatic licensing, often necessary to administer the importation of goods where SPS- and TBT-related related issues are of particular importance. Some quantitative restrictions, such as quotas, prohibitions, and export restraints, are currently in place but largely limited to a number of sensitive products.

Among non-technical measures, preshipment inspections affect about 20 percent of trade and products. Although such inspections may be necessary to provide some assurance of the quality or quantity of the shipment, thus facilitating international trade, they do add to the cost of trading.

Price control measures (which apply to 5 percent of trade and only 2 percent of products) are one of the least used forms of NTMs. These measures affect only a small share of goods and are largely related to anti-dumping and countervailing duties, as well as some forms of administrative pricing for staple food and energy or other sensitive sectors.

The incidence of different forms of NTMs varies across geographic areas. Figure 1.3 illustrates the use of NTMs by differentiating the countries in the sample in three broad developing regions and a high income group. Although SPS and TBT are the most used forms of NTMs, independent of the region, many countries, especially in Asia and Latin America, still implement a large number of quantitative restrictions (mostly in the form of licensing). African countries appear to regulate their imports relatively more than many other developing countries, especially in relation to preshipment inspection (PSI). The reason behind this relatively large number of PSI measures is that these are often implemented to fight corruption, to facilitate and accelerate custom procedures, and ultimately to help in the correct evaluation of imports and their proper taxation. Moreover the large use of SPS and TBT by African countries may result from an effort to harmonize regulations with their main trading partner, the European Union.

The use of NTMs varies considerably not only across regions but even more so across countries (figure 1.4). On average, countries apply some form of NTM for slightly less than half of the about 5,000 products included in the HS 6-digit classification. This figure varies greatly by country; for example, in Africa, Tanzania and Senegal use NTMs substantially less than Kenya or Uganda. In Latin America, Argentina's use of NTMs is double that of Chile or Paraguay. In Asia, Bangladesh and the Philippines use NTMs much more than Cambodia or Indonesia. Although this large variance may be due to some extent to different primary data collection methods, it is likely to explain only part of the differences, as a large variance is also found for Latin American countries whose data were collected by the same agency, ALADI (*Asociación Latinoamericana de Integración*).

Similar conclusions can be reached by examining coverage ratios (the percentage of imports subject to NTMs) as these are found to be highly correlated with frequency indices. Although correlated, coverage ratios

Figure 1.3 Frequency Index and Coverage Ratios by Region and Chapter of NTM

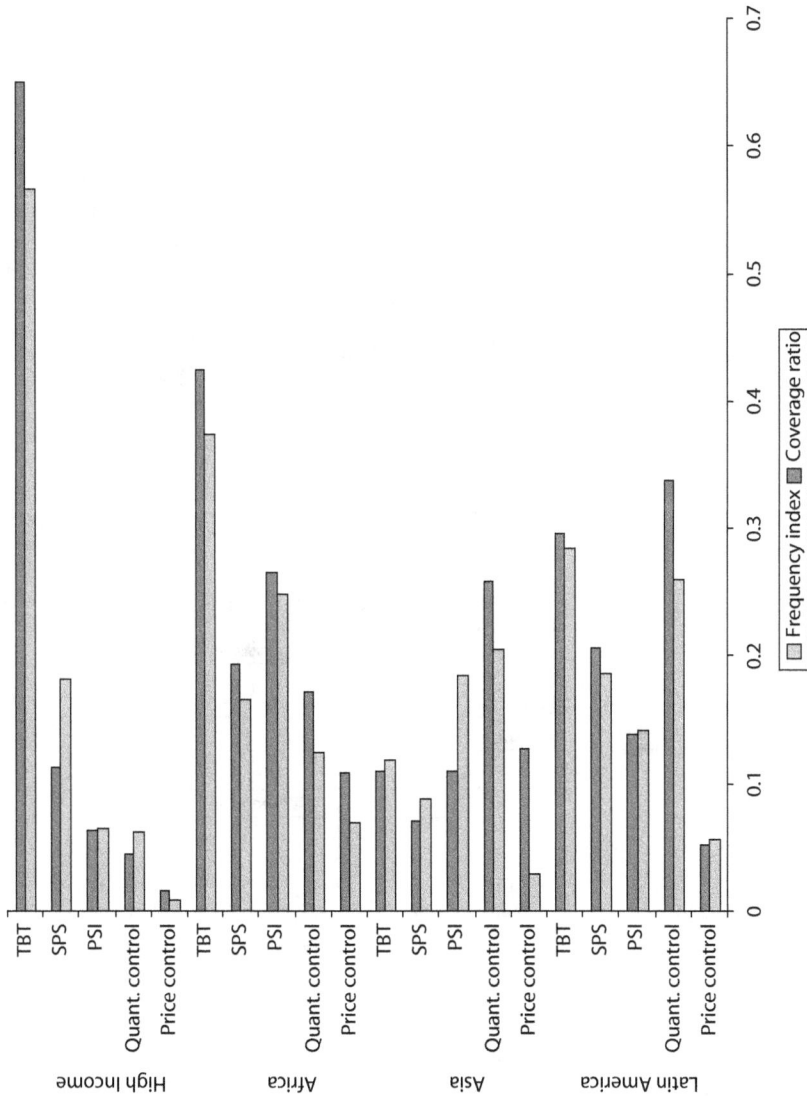

Source: Gourdon and Nicita 2012.

Figure 1.4   Frequency Indices and Coverage Ratios, by Country

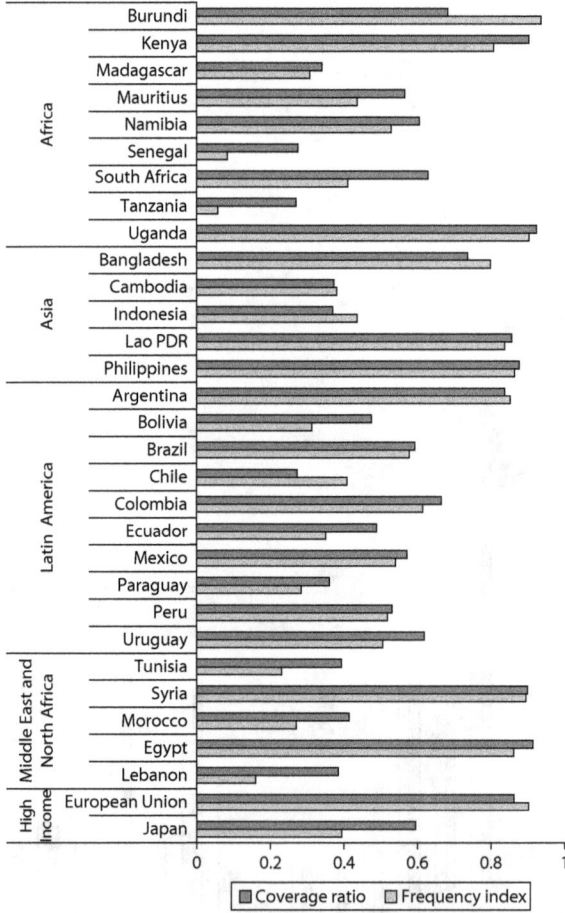

Source: Gourdon and Nicita 2012.

are often lower than frequency indices. This is possibly due to the endo-geneity issue (NTMs may restrict trade and this will downwardly bias the coverage ratio). The problem of endogeneity seems to be supported by the relatively lower coverage ratio for Latin American countries, where measures imposing quantity restrictions are still significant. The differ-ence between the two incidence measures is particularly striking for Tanzania (from 5 to 30 percent) and Lebanon (from 15 to 40 percent). A coverage ratio relatively higher than a frequency index can be explained by two factors. The first is import composition. Countries, especially low-income countries, often import larger volumes of products where NTMs are more extensively used (agriculture). The second factor is a larger use of NTM policies on products that are most traded (for example, for consumer protection). This is often the case in developed countries.

The distribution of NTMs across sectors does not vary substantially across countries, especially with regard to SPS and TBT measures, as it reflects the technical properties of products rather than economic policy choices. While more than 60 percent of food-related products are found to be affected by at least one form of SPS, TBTs can be applied to a much wider set of products and more uniformly applied across economic sectors, with their number peaks in textiles, footwear, processed food, and chemicals. Preshipment inspections are widely used in Sub-Saharan Africa, while in other regions they are limited to food products and textiles, apparel, and footwear. Price control measures are mainly administrative pricing, anti-dumping, and countervailing duties used as trade defensive policies; thus, by their nature they are applied only to specific products such as some food products and to textiles and apparel in Latin America. In addition, price-control measures are more concentrated in agricultural products, textiles, and footwear. Finally, quantity control measures are applied more or less uniformly across economic sectors, with peaks in agricultural goods and animal products, motor vehicles, and chemical products. These are sectors where particularly sensitive products are often regulated by non-automatic licenses, quotas, and sometimes outright prohibitions.

Data Caveats
The above analysis must be nuanced, given some issues regarding data measurement, including the following:

- The ability to classify a law or regulation into the appropriate NTM category is only part of the challenge in assembling an NTM database. A big challenge is that most countries do not have a unique repository of NTM data at the national level since laws and regulations affecting trade are often promulgated by different government agencies and regulatory bodies. In practice, the data must be carefully scrutinized for duplications, omissions, or other problems in order to minimize inaccuracies.

- There is a risk of double counting when a principal NTM is implemented through another NTM; both must be notified at least once to the WTO. For example, tariff-rate quotas (TRQs) for agricultural products are often administered through an import licensing procedure, where the former needs to be notified to the Committee on Agriculture and the latter to the Committee on Import Licensing. Likewise, import licensing is often a side measure associated with SPS and TBT measures. This means that import licensing may simply be a "secondary" measure supporting the principal measure. If such secondary measures are reported separately, as is foreseen in the WTO notification requirements, this creates problems of double counting, which would need to be addressed when an aggregation of measures across different subject areas is undertaken.

Views from the Business Sector

Firm surveys across the world highlight private-sector demands for more transparency in the adoption and application of NTMs across countries. Surveys and face-to-face interviews suggest that a primary concern of the private sector in poor countries (and other countries as well), particularly of small and medium-sized enterprises, is the lack of visibility of NTMs. Information on what regulations are applied, by whom, and for what products is hard to get because in every destination country, it is scattered over many ministries and agencies. Even inside governments, agencies may communicate poorly, resulting in a lack of coordination and coherence of regulatory regimes. This makes it particularly difficult to make efficient business decisions for firms without the capability, the scale of operations, or the long-term relationships needed to find their way in regulatory mazes. Regulations also tend to change with little warning, creating another source of uncertainty that hurts small producers and those located in poor countries more than others. The business sector is increasingly concerned about non-tariff obstacles to trade, which are less visible and more complex than tariff protection.

From the perspective of the business sector, non-tariff measures increase the trade-related costs, making their products less competitive in the destination market. In cases where an NTM is used for protectionist reasons, the associated costs are even higher. The increase in costs resulting from applying an NTM penalizes not only producers in the exporting country but also businesses and final consumers in the importing country. Technical regulations and product standards, for example, can increase the costs of compliance in two ways. On one hand, they can impose additional fixed costs on exporters who have to adapt products to the specific standards and regulations applied by the importing country. On the other hand, conformity assessment procedures, such as testing to demonstrate compliance with these technical measures, may induce additional costs.

As part of the MAST initiative, a company-level survey with 300 to 400 face-to-face interviews was carried out in order to identify at the product level those measures that exporting companies perceive as barriers in their daily business, as well as the reasons why companies experience a measure as burdensome. The following analysis is based on the survey results for five countries: Chile, the Philippines, Thailand, Tunisia, and Uganda (table 1.1).

The ITC/UNCTAD survey results indicate that the majority of NTMs that exporters experienced as non-tariff barriers concern technical measures, which account for about 73 percent on average per surveyed country. These measures include, among others, regulations related to product characteristics or the related production process.

For exporters, it can be challenging to comply with these regulations, as they might be very complex and often vary significantly by country and region. Certification requirements, which refer in particular to the verification of the conformity of products with technical regulations, are a major concern for the surveyed exporters, no matter which region is the destination for their product—with the exception of Africa (figure 1.5). For goods exported to African countries, as well as to Latin America and the Caribbean, the share of barriers related to customs formalities is much higher than for the goods shipped to other regions (22 percent and 15 percent, respectively). At the same time, the shares of obstacles to

Table 1.1   NTMs Experienced by Exporting Companies as NTBs
percent

NTM group	Chile	Philippines	Thailand	Tunisia	Uganda	Average[a]
Technical measures (e.g., product characteristics requirement, production process, conformity assessment)	70.3	76.4	93.5	62.7	64.1	73.4
Preshipment inspection and other customs formalities	14.0	3.1	2.3	22.6	23.1	13.0
Licenses, quotas, and other quantity control measures	6.1	0.4	2.2	0.5	0.3	1.9
Charges, taxes, and other para-tariff measures	1.2	2.7	0.2	4.7	7.4	3.2
Finance measures regulating access to and cost of foreign exchange for imports and defining payment terms	2.1	0.6	0.1	4.2	0.2	1.4
Other	6.4	16.9	1.6	5.3	4.9	7.0
Total	100.0	100.0	100.0	100.0	100.0	100.0

Source: Mimouni, Averbeck, and Skorobogatova 2009.
a. Simple cross-country average.

Figure 1.5   Seven Most Prevailing Types of NTMs Experienced by Surveyed Companies as NTBs, by Regional Destination

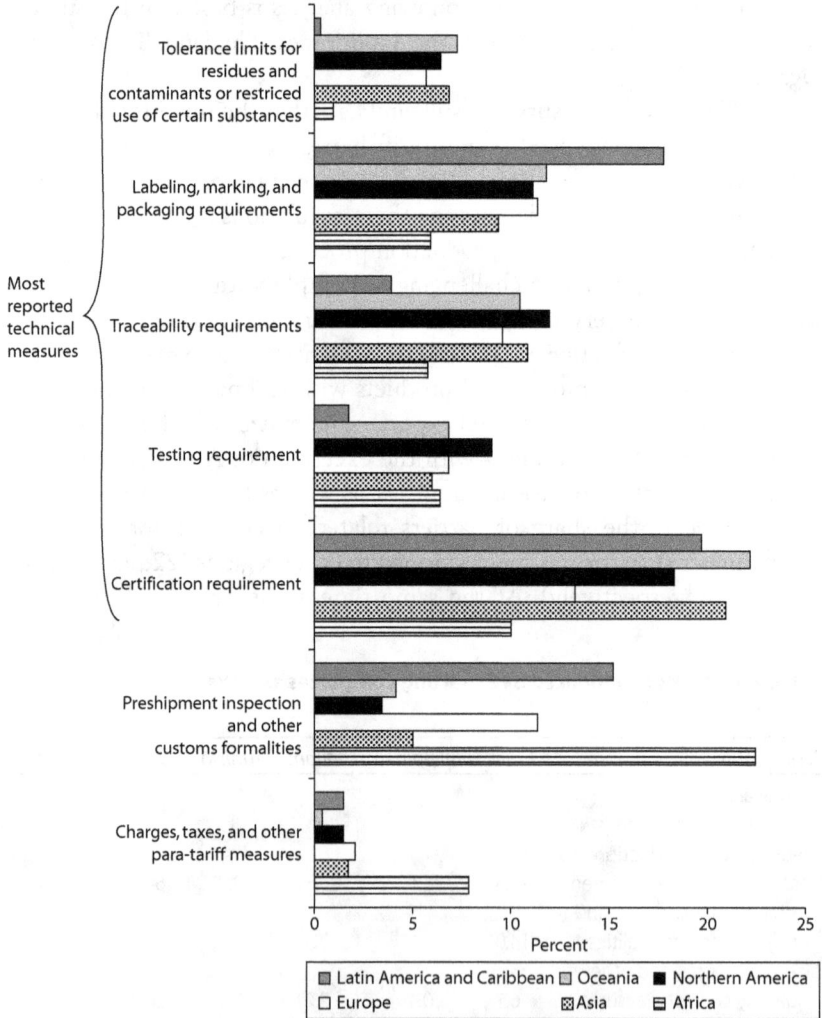

Source: Mimouni, Averbeck, and Skorobogatova 2009.

trade experienced in relation to traceability requirements and tolerance limits for residues and contaminants or restricted use of certain substances are very low in these two regions. The share of testing requirements is also very low when goods are bound for Africa (2 percent against 6 percent on average).

The survey data also reveal that in the case of Chile, Thailand, and Uganda, and to a lesser extent Tunisia, NTBs are much more prevailing when trading within a region. Chile, for example, mainly exports to the Asia-Pacific region, but most of the reported cases concern Latin American and Caribbean countries.[2] Almost 38 percent of total Chilean export is destined for Asia-Pacific, but only 8 percent of all reported cases are related to this region. The situation is opposite in Chile's home region: no more than 14 percent of export is regional, but 43 percent of all obstacles concern Latin American and Caribbean countries. In the case of Uganda, 44 percent of exports are bound for African countries. Uganda's neighboring countries— Democratic Republic of Congo, Kenya, Rwanda, and Sudan—account for more than 40 percent of all reported trade barriers, despite existing trade agreements. This can be partly explained by the fact that Uganda is a landlocked country and Ugandan exporters have to comply with both transit country requirements and the requirements imposed by countries of final export destination.

Although the obstacles to trade are mainly related to measures faced on the export market, these may not necessarily cause the problems and challenges the exporters complain about. The problems faced by the surveyed companies refer to weak customs and administrative procedures, a lack of local facilities and infrastructure, and insufficient capacity within their own country. That is, the exporters may face difficulties in complying with technical regulations because of the lack of infrastructure or efficiency in their own country.

Living Up to International Commitments

International commitments to increase transparency and improve regulations are important to ensure the predictability of the business environment, as well as to identify and address unintended obstacles to trade. International commitments can also serve as a check against subtle forms of protectionism. Accordingly, regulatory transparency has been at the forefront of the international trade agenda at the multilateral, bilateral, and regional levels. It appears even more topical during the current economic crisis when pressing calls for emergency action can lead to intended or unintended protectionist measures that do not undergo the scrutiny and accountability provided by transparent rule-making processes (Moise 2011).

Regulatory reform and trade liberalization play complementary roles in that they enhance competition to give consumers and businesses competitive, non-discriminatory access to a wider selection of inputs and final goods in domestic markets. These processes facilitate both (1) international trade to enhance foreign market access for domestic goods and the entry of capital goods and (2) investment on more favorable terms, which expands productive capacity, generates employment, and favors the diffusion of new technologies. They also contribute to the development of efficient regulation that reduces the costs of market entry and operation in general.

The WTO and OECD are the main international bodies that provide guidelines for NTMs and regulations. The WTO addresses the NTM agenda through both the transparency obligation and the guidelines to reconcile governments' policy objectives with the requirement that the regulations do not restrict trade unnecessarily or are used purposely for protectionist measures. The OECD advocates for key efficiency principles for regulations in general.

Because transparency at both the multilateral and national levels is essential to the smooth operation of international trade agreements, and more broadly to the good functioning of the multilateral trading system, the "Agreement Establishing the World Trade Organization" (hereafter, WTO Agreement) includes multiple transparency provisions.[3] These provisions can be grouped into five categories: (1) goods and services schedules of concessions, (2) the Trade Policy Review Mechanism, (3) publication and notification requirements, (4) internal transparency of the institution toward its members, and (5) external transparency of the institution toward civil society. The first three categories cover provisions that ensure the transparency of national policies, which in the area of trade in goods can be roughly divided into two groups: tariffs and NTMs.

WTO Guiding Principles

NTMs exist within a framework established by the rules of the trading system, including the multilateral rules of the WTO Agreement, the rules in regional trade agreements, and even rules agreed in bilateral or plurilateral negotiations. The following section discusses these rules and their connection to the empirical analysis of NTMs and their effects.

Legal rules provide an agreed normative benchmark for NTMs' acceptability. By characterizing some NTMs as illegal, they define which NTMs a government is obligated to address—and its trading partners have a right to complain about. Conversely, where an NTM is not characterized as illegal under the rules, trading partners and their stakeholders who seek action to reduce its trade-reducing effects can only obtain it if the importing country agrees. Thus, the rules draw the line between actions that trading partners can expect for free and actions for which they must negotiate and pay in some form.

Substantively, these rules require non-discriminatory treatment, and they permit member governments to maintain whatever level of protection they desire, but they do not stop at non-discrimination. They also require that regulations must be necessary to achieve a legitimate policy objective, and not just be disguised barriers to trade or unnecessarily restrictive of trade. Where the WTO rules stop, negotiations begin; governments have undertaken higher-than-WTO levels of discipline in regional trade agreements or through bilateral arrangements, or they have unilaterally liberalized NTMs when viewed as in the national economic interest. Although regulatory disciplines cover different trade dimensions, such as services as well as licensing procedures and others, the discussion focuses on general obligations, and in particular, the WTO disciplines on SPS measures and TBTs as examples of international regulations for NTMs.

Background. The General Agreement on Tariffs and Trade (GATT) basic rules for regulation are limited to requirements not to discriminate and not to ban or restrict imports. However, the drafters recognized a short list of policies that would trump trade liberalization—some of which are relevant to NTMs. GATT expanded discipline on regulation through the 1979 "Agreement on Technical Barriers to Trade" (TBT Agreement), a plurilateral code that added some rules affecting even non-discriminatory regulations. Finally, after the Uruguay Round of trade negotiations (1995), the WTO agreement included an amended TBT Agreement as well as a new "Agreement on the Application of Sanitary and Phyto-Sanitary Measures" (SPS Agreement). These two agreements go well beyond non-discrimination, and provide additional discipline on NTMs.

GATT was designed as a multilateral tariff agreement, with non-tariff obligations designed to secure the value of the agreed tariff concessions and to generalize their benefit to all GATT members on a most-favored nation basis. It is self-evident that a discriminatory internal tax or regulation can eliminate any benefit of a tariff binding. For this reason, the GATT recognizes the principle that internal taxes, charges, and regulations should not be applied to imported or domestic products so as to protect domestic production (Article III:1); however, it prohibits the imposition of internal taxes or charges on imported products that are higher than those imposed on like domestic products (Article III:2). Article III:4 requires that imported products be accorded "treatment no less favorable than that accorded to like products of domestic origin in respect of all laws, regulations and requirements affecting their internal sale, offering for sale, purchase, transportation or use." As a GATT panel described in 1958, "the intention of the drafters of the Agreement was clearly to treat the imported products in the same way as the like domestic products once they had been cleared through Customs. Otherwise indirect protection could be given" (GATT 1958, para.11).[4]

In dispute settlement decisions interpreting Article III:4, GATT panels clarified that the scope of this provision is very broad indeed, but it intended to cover not only the laws and regulations that directly govern the conditions of sale or purchase but also any laws or regulations that might adversely affect the conditions of competition between the domestic and imported products on the domestic market (GATT 1958, para. 12). In later decisions, panels clarified that this non-discrimination requirement applied to technical regulations, government benefits, sales practices of state-owned enterprises, regulations on product quality or ingredients, measures discouraging use of certain products, labeling regulations, and shipping charges of government-run railways or postal services (WTO 1995, 173–82).

In principle, the trade effects of an NTM are not important in determining whether it violates these non-discrimination rules. Since 1949 it has been recognized that any higher taxation of imported products violates Article III, even if no damage is shown, and even if there is no tariff binding on the product in question. As a GATT panel found in 1987, the prohibition on tax discrimination between like products does not protect expectations of any particular trade volume, but expectations on the competitive relationship between imported and domestic products (WTO 1995, 128).

GATT/WTO Exceptions for Discriminatory NTMs. The GATT[5] includes a short list of exceptions in Article XX, which permit a government to maintain measures that would otherwise violate the positive rules of the GATT—for instance, measures that discriminate against or between imports or ban importation of a good. The Article XX exceptions permit measures necessary for, or related to, certain named policies—for instance, measures "necessary to protect human, animal or plant life or health," measures "necessary to protect public morals," measures "necessary to secure compliance" with otherwise GATT-consistent laws and regulations, or measures "relating to the conservation of natural resources if such measures are made effective in conjunction with restrictions on domestic production or consumption." A proviso to the list requires that the measures in question not be "applied in a manner which would constitute a means of arbitrary or unjustifiable discrimination between countries where the same conditions prevail, or a disguised restriction on international trade." In any dispute, the complaining party has the burden of proof on whether the positive rules have been violated; however, exceptions are an affirmative defense, for which the burden shifts to the defending party.

For a given NTM, then, a trading partner must demonstrate a rule violation (for instance, denial of national treatment). The importing country then must show that the measure falls within the policy objectives listed in Article XX. It must show that the application of the measure does not discriminate arbitrarily between countries where relevant conditions are the same and that it also takes into account relevant differences. It must also demonstrate that the measure is not a form of disguised protectionism.

Necessity figures in three of the Article XX General Exceptions, and dispute settlement panels have relied on a balancing approach in analyzing necessity. In the leading WTO case analyzing a discriminatory Korean regime for imported beef, the Appellate Body noted that claims of necessity must be evaluated in relation to the circumstances, and that this evaluation involves in every case a process of weighing and balancing a series of factors, which prominently include (1) the actual contribution made by the measure to achieving the stated objective within Article XX, (2) the importance of the common interests or values protected, and (3) the restrictive impact of the measure on trade (*Korea–Beef*, para 164) (WTO 2001).

In *Korea–Beef* and other cases, the WTO Appellate Body looked for a relationship between the measure and the end pursued that was not just a contribution to accomplishing the objective, but was closer to being indispensable to accomplishing that objective. The party seeking to demonstrate that its measures are necessary must establish this through evidence or data establishing that the measure actually contributes to the achievement of the objectives pursued. Evaluation of a measure's necessity also requires an evaluation of its restrictive effect on trade (or on behind-the-border sale or distribution of imports, if the issue is justifying behind-the-border discriminatory regulations). The less restrictive an NTM is, the more likely it is to be justifiable as "necessary" (*China–Publications*, WTO 2010, para. 305–10).

In the WTO *Korea–Beef* and *US–Gambling* cases, the Appellate Body clarified that as a panel evaluates necessity, it must examine whether the defending party could reasonably be expected to employ an alternative measure that is WTO-consistent (or less WTO-inconsistent) that would achieve the objectives pursued by the measure at issue. An alternative measure may be not "reasonably available" where it is merely theoretical in nature, or where it imposes an undue burden on a member, such as prohibitive costs or technical difficulties in its implementation. Moreover, an alternative measure that is "reasonably available" must preserve the defending party's right to achieve its desired level of protection with respect to the objective pursued under Article XX. Where the complaining party identifies an alternative measure, the defending party has the burden of demonstrating that its GATT-inconsistent measure is "necessary" (*China–Publications*, WTO 2010, para. 319).

To determine whether such an alternative measure exists, then, the panel must evaluate whether (a) the measure is economically and technically feasible, (b) the alternative would achieve the same objectives as the original measure, and (c) it is less trade restrictive than the measure analyzed. If any of these elements is not met, the alternative measure is deemed to be not compatible with WTO obligations.

The SPS and TBT Agreements. The WTO SPS and TBT Agreements go beyond the GATT and address the impact on trade of even non-discriminatory NTMs.[6] Specifically, the SPS tackles typical NTMs affecting food trade and applies only to SPS measures. The TBT Agreement provides related but separate disciplines and applies to all other standards, technical regulations, and conformity assessment procedures for all products.[7]

The SPS Agreement presents the tradeoff between free trade and regulatory sovereignty most explicitly. It states that WTO members have the right to take SPS measures, but requires that such measures be applied only to the extent necessary to protect human, animal, or plant life or health, and that the measures be based on scientific principles and not maintained without sufficient scientific evidence (Articles 2.1–2.2) Whether scientific evidence supports a measure is an element of whether the measure is necessary and proportional. A member has the right to set its desired "appropriate level of sanitary or phytosanitary protection," but in doing so it must take into account the objective of minimizing negative trade effects (Article 5.4).

The TBT Agreement confronts the same tradeoff in similar terms. It requires that members ensure that technical regulations are not prepared, adopted, or applied with a view to, or with the effect of, creating unnecessary obstacles to trade. It further clarifies that technical regulations must not be more trade-restrictive than necessary to fulfill a legitimate objective, taking into account the risks of non-fulfillment. Unlike GATT Article XX, which is limited to a short list of acceptable excuses such as public morality and public health, TBT Article 2.2 provides an open illustrative list of acceptable "legitimate objectives."

These SPS and TBT necessity requirements encourage members to address non-trade problems such as product safety through less trade-reducing and more efficient measures. Thus, the costs in terms of trade inherent in the regulations should be clearly lower than the benefits obtained. These agreements promote a more efficient use of instruments that create fewer distortions from an economic standpoint.

The analysis of necessity under the SPS and TBT Agreements rolls together the same combination of themes as the analysis of necessity in GATT Article XX: (1) a measure's contribution toward a policy objective, (2) the legitimacy and importance of the objective pursued, and (3) the measure's restrictive impact on trade (including the government's choice not to employ reasonably available alternatives that would have been less restrictive). There is an essential difference, however. In any dispute applying SPS Article 2.2, 5.4, or 5.6 to a (non-discriminatory) SPS measure, or a dispute applying TBT Article 2.2 to any other measure, the complaining party bears the burden of proving there is a lack of necessity. On the other hand, in a GATT dispute where the defending party invokes an affirmative defense under Article XX, that party has the burden of proof on all the issues in Article XX (including necessity, and non-discriminatory, non-protectionist application). This difference can make a substantial difference in the outcome of the dispute

Panels have not found difficulty in applying this three-part test, relying on objective evidence from experts on the risks combated by the SPS measures at issue—for instance, fish diseases (in *Australia–Salmon*, WTO 1998), or plant diseases and plant quarantine (*Japan–Apples*, WTO 2003). Since the alternative measures proposed by exporting countries will always be significantly less restrictive than the status quo, the only question is whether the proposed alternative is technically and economically feasible and would deliver the importing country's designated "appropriate level of protection" (ALOP). As the Appellate Body noted, the SPS Agreement does not explicitly require a member to define its ALOPs routinely for all products; but in a dispute, the panel must use some benchmark for applying SPS obligations, and if the defending party does not supply an ALOP, the panel will simply have to infer it from the level of protection in its actual SPS measures (WTO 1998, para. 205–07). In the compliance phase of the *Salmon* and *Apples* disputes, each panel relied on its experts and quickly concluded that the importing country's amended import regime failed the three-part test.

OECD Regulatory Guiding Principles

The OECD Efficient Regulation Principles provide guidance to policy makers designing and implementing rules and regulations, including those that may impact trade and firms' competitiveness. According to the OECD, countries that progress simultaneously with market opening and regulatory reform policies are better placed to take advantage of the benefits of trade liberalization. The OECD also recognizes the benefits of regulatory reform, which is about improving regulation, not necessarily through less regulation. The key benefits of regulatory reform are threefold:

- *Improvement in efficiency of the domestic economy and in the ability to adapt to change.* Better regulation leads to lower costs for business, higher productivity, more investment, and greater innovation. This contributes to more job creation, higher growth, and an increase in size of the private sector, while delivering lower prices, improved quality, and wider choices to consumers.
- *Improved competitiveness in international and domestic markets.* Inefficient regulations can constrain the ability of domestic firms to diversify and compete abroad and at home. A better regulatory environment will also tend to make a country more attractive for both domestic and international investment.
- *Public policy goals are more effectively and efficiently achieved.* The objective of regulation is to achieve public policy goals such as health and safety. A key outcome of regulatory reform is *to improve the effectiveness with which such goals are achieved while reducing the burden on* firms in complying with the regulations.

The "Efficient Regulation Principles of the OECD" are summarized in nine points:

1. *Transparency and openness.* All stakeholders (including existing firms, new firms, potential entrants, foreign firms, all government

departments concerned, and consumers) should have easy access to information about regulations and procedures and be given the opportunity to participate in consultations regarding regulations. In practice, excessive discretion by field-level bureaucrats should be avoided and there should be procedures whereby stakeholders can appeal the decisions of bureaucrats.

2. *Non-discrimination.* There should be equality of competitive opportunities between like products and services irrespective of their country of origin. In the parlance of the GATT this requires both national treatment and MFN (most favored nation) treatment and applies to rules and regulations that are more onerous for domestic producers than for importers.

3. *Avoidance of unnecessary trade restrictiveness.* Governments should use regulations that are not more trade- and investment-restrictive than necessary to fulfill the legitimate public policy objectives. This requires careful assessment of the impact of regulations so that in neither design nor implementation do they create unjustified difficulties for the free flow of goods, services, and investment.

4. *Use* of *performance-based regulations* (rather than design or descriptive characteristics). It is easier and less costly when firms have flexibility to meet requirements as this allows for innovation and improved efficiency. Also, where feasible, consider alternatives to regulation such as financial measures (taxes, subsidies) or other market measures (market institutions, defining property rights).

5. *Use of regulatory impact analysis* (RIA) to assess the need for new regulation and to review the impact of existing regulations.[8]

6. *Administrative simplification* to minimize the administrative burdens on firms in complying with regulations. Initiatives that can contribute to this objective include one stop shops, information technology–driven mechanisms, simplification of license and permit procedures, and setting time limits for decision-making.

7. *Use of internationally harmonized measures* to minimize the burdens on firms that come from having to comply with different standards and regulations for like products in international trade. National authorities should systematically examine whether a relevant international standard

exists when proposing or reviewing a regulation and, if so, whether it would be appropriate and effective for the regulation.

8. *Ensurance that the quality of conformity assessment procedures.* Conformity assessment procedures can facilitate trade by increasing consumer confidence if done without excessive time and cost. But conformity assessment procedures can raise barriers when there is a duplication of costs in different markets for essentially identical tests against the same or equivalent standards. Options include mutual recognition agreements, recognition of supplier's declaration of conformity, unilateral recognition of conformity assessment results from other countries, and voluntary agreements between conformity assessment bodies in different countries.

9. *Incorporation of competition principles into regulatory practices.* Increasing competition should be recognized as a goal of regulatory reform such that there should be mechanisms to identify anticompetitive practices and to address complaints from consumers and new or potential firm entrants.

Preferential Liberalization and Regional Commitments

While the various agreements under WTO set out general rules for the design and implementation of product standards, the main instruments of liberalization in this area have been deployed mostly in regional contexts. Duplication of testing procedures among member countries is frequent and does not add value to a product, but does add to the cost of compliance. Obtaining approvals is a lengthy process that involves substantial documentation and tedious bureaucratic procedures. While technical regulations generate important compliance costs, the lack of regional coordination may carry significant additional costs. A unique feature of preferential liberalization is that it offers an alternative means, complementary to multilateral efforts, of diminishing, through bilateral mutual recognition and harmonization efforts, the costs associated with compliance with standards. This feature and the presumption that standards are not necessarily established for protectionist purposes suggest that preferential liberalization can be a force for good.

Regional initiatives are not free of risk with regard to their compatibility with the broader aim of multilateral liberalization. For example, preferential agreements involving both developed and developing countries

(North–South Preferential Trade Agreements) can lead to specifications that many developing countries find overly complex or burdensome. Indeed, these countries could perceive these agreements as locking them out of vital international markets (Baldwin 2000). It is therefore important for policy makers and trade policy practitioners to understand the issues that product standards raise in a regional integration context and, in particular, the challenges developing countries can face in dealing with foreign standards as they become increasingly integrated into the world economy.

Finally, coordination among countries in implementing their standards policies may yield harmonized policies, reducing the cost of market access while preserving regulatory objectives. A potential difficulty with this kind of coordination is its assumption that it is optimal for the same standard to apply across a wide range of countries. In fact, however, different economic and social conditions may call for different standards (Maur and Shepherd 2011)

A review of the practice of addressing TBT and SPS measures in preferential trade agreements (PTAs) suggests these agreements should include, where feasible, a number of important best-practice provisions to ensure that agreements converge with, and support, the multilateral trading system (Stoler 2011):

1. *Adopt international standards.* The parties to the PTA should undertake to use international standards whenever possible, as doing so guarantees a high level of protection in the integrated market and makes it easier for third parties to trade in that market.

2. *Limit harmonization to essential health and safety standards.* If the parties to the PTA decide on an approach of harmonizing their standards and conformity assessment procedures, they should accept that it might be necessary to limit harmonization to essential health and safety standards and rely on mutual recognition and equivalence techniques for other areas.

3. *Plan for technical assistance and capacity-building for the less developed partners.* If one partner is less developed than the other, the PTA should incorporate technical assistance and capacity-building measures to assist the institutions and exporters of the developing-country partner. In negotiating a PTA, governments should recognize that deeper integration and the resolution of standards-related problems will take

time and will require considerable bilateral work. A PTA that aims to be effective should incorporate bilateral institutions (committees and the like) that have a mandate to deal with standards-related questions over time through harmonization, equivalence, or mutual recognition techniques. Ideally, the institutions established in the PTA should also be capable of helping to resolve trade-related problems arising out of exporters' need to comply with private standards in an importing country's market.

4. **Eliminate duplication for the same products.** If technical regulations and conformity assessment procedures cannot be harmonized, it is important for the purposes of the PTA that the parties work to elimi-nate duplicate or multiple measures or mandatory tests for the same product. This is particularly crucial for small and medium-size enter-prises that cannot afford the high cost of meeting differing regulations and testing regimes. Mutual recognition agreements are important tools in this respect.

5. **Consult with partners on new regulations.** Transparency regarding SPS standards in international trade is very important for businesses and consumers. PTA partners should consider enacting WTO+ notification obligations and a commitment not to implement any technical regula-tion or SPS measure until it has been published and comments from the PTA partners have been taken into account.

6. **Adopt a work program.** The PTA should be a living agreement with a commitment to a work plan or to prioritization of problem resolution through harmonization, mutual recognition, equivalence measures, and other policy tools that enable elimination or mitigation of trade-related problems over time. Ideally, the work program should also be capable of addressing problems relating to compliance with private standards.

7. **PTA provisions on TBT and SPS matters should be legally binding.** Through a judicious combination of soft and hard law, the agreement should be negotiated to provide a pathway that permits an evolution and deepening of integration over time by allowing the gradual resolu-tion of TBT and SPS issues in the bilateral relationship. Such a pathway should be considered an integral part of any PTA that aims to deal effectively with standards, certification, and conformity assessment

problems. Eventual recourse to the PTA dispute settlement provisions should be an option, in addition to recourse to the WTO Dispute Settlement Understanding.

8. ***Commit to open regionalism.*** PTA parties should agree to an overall commitment whereby technical regulations and conformity assessment procedures are always applied on a national treatment basis. Third parties whose technical regulations and conformity assessment procedures can be demonstrated as being equivalent to the level agreed to by the PTA partners should be permitted to benefit from the arrangements between the partners. A commitment to open regionalism would help to ensure that PTAs support the multilateral system.

Notes

1. The Multi-Agency Support Team (MAST) comprises members from the following organizations: Food and Agriculture Organization of the United Nations (FAO), International Monetary Fund (IMF), International Trade Centre (ITC), Organisation for Economic Co-operation and Development (OECD), United Nations Conference on Trade and Development (UNCTAD), United Nations Industrial Development Organization (UNIDO), World Bank, and World Trade Organization (WTO).

2. The analysis of the regional distribution of trade obstacles reported by Chilean exporters is based on the top-20 export destinations, representing 88 percent of the total Chilean export value (based on UNSD Comtrade 2007 data). These export destinations have been categorized into geographic regions, namely Africa, Asia, Europe, Latin America and the Caribbean, Northern America, and Oceania. Similar calculations were performed for each surveyed country.

3. This section is based on Cadot, Maliszewska, and Sáez (2011).

4. The panel in this case comprised trade officials who had participated in the negotiation of the GATT in 1946–48.

5. This section is based on Cadot, Maliszewska, and Sáez (2011).

6. This section is based on Cadot, Maliszewska, and Sáez (2011).

7. SPS Article 1.1 provides that the SPS Agreement applies to all SPS measures that may, directly or indirectly, affect international trade; Annex A defines the scope of SPS measures subject to the agreement (health protection measures, principally to protect against risks arising from entry; establishment or spread of pests or diseases; or additives, contaminants, or toxins in food, beverages, or feedstuffs). The TBT Agreement applies to all technical regulations, standards,

and conformity assessment schemes *except* for SPS measures—for instance, food regulations imposed for other reasons.

8. A typical RIA includes the following: purpose and nature of the regulation; the consultation process; review of options for solving the problem; benefits and costs of the regulation; compliance, enforcement, and monitoring; and summary and recommendations.

References

Bacchetta, Marc, Jürgen Richtering, and Roy Santana. 2012. "How Much Light Do WTO Notifications Shed on NTMs?" In *Non-Tariff Measures—A Fresh Look at Trade Policy's New Frontier,* ed. Olivier Cadot and Mariem Malouche. London/Washington, DC: Centre for Economic Policy Research/World Bank.

Baldwin, Richard. 2000. "Regulatory Protectionism, Developing Nations, and a Two-Tier World Trade System," CEPR Discussion Paper No. 2574, London.

Cadot, Olivier, Maryla Maliszewska, and Sebastián Sáez. 2011. "Non-Tariff Measures: Impact, Regulation, and Trade Facilitation." In *Border Management Modernization,* ed. Gerard McLinden, Enrique Fanta, David Widdowson, and Tom Doyle. Washington DC: World Bank.

GATT (General Agreement on Tariffs and Trade). 1958. Italian Discrimination Against Imported Agricultural Machinery. Panel report adopted on October 23, 1958, reprinted in GATT Basic Instruments and Selected Documents, 7th Supplement, p. 60.

Gourdon, Julien, and Alessandro Nicita. 2012. "Non-Tariff Measures: Evidence from Recent Data Collection." In *Non-Tariff Measures—A Fresh Look at Trade Policy's New Frontier,* ed. Olivier Cadot and Mariem Malouche. London/Washington, DC: Centre for Economic Policy Research/World Bank.

MAST (Multi-Agency Support Team). 2009. "Report to the Group of Eminent Persons on Non-Tariff Barriers." Presented at the Group's meeting of November 5, 2009. United Nations Conference on Trade and Development, Geneva, Switzerland.

Maur, Jean-Christophe, and Ben Shepherd. 2011. "Product Standards." In *Preferential Trade Agreement: Policies for Development,* ed. Jean-Pierre Chauffour and Jean-Christophe Maur. Washington, DC: World Bank.

Mimouni, Mondher, Carolin Averbeck, and Olga Skorobogatova. 2009. "Obstacles to Trade from the Perspective of the Business Sector: A Cross-Country Comparison." In *The Global Enabling Trade Report,* ed. Robert Z. Lawrence, Margareta Drzeniek Hanouz, and John Moavenzadeh, 69–76. Geneva: World Economic Forum.

Stoler, Andrew L. "TBT and SPS Measures, in Practice." In *Preferential Trade Agreement: Policies for Development*, ed. Jean-Pierre Chauffour and Jean-Christophe Maur. Washington, DC: World Bank.

UNCTAD (United Nations Conference on Trade and Development). 2010. "Non-Tariff Measures: Evidence from Selected Developing Countries and Future Research Agenda." Developing Countries in International Trade Studies, New York and Geneva, United Nations.

WTO (World Trade Organization). 1995. Analytical Index/Guide to GATT Law and Practice.

———. 1998. Panel Report, *Australia – Measures Affecting Importation of Salmon*, WT/DS18/R and Corr.1, adopted 6 November 1998, as modified by Appellate Body Report WT/DS18/AB/R, DSR 1998:VIII, 3407

———. 2001. Appellate Body Report, *Korea – Measures Affecting Imports of Fresh, Chilled and Frozen Beef.* WT/DS161/AB/R, WT/DS169/AB/R, adopted 10 January 2001, DSR 2001:I, 5.

———. 2003. Panel Report, *Japan – Measures Affecting the Importation of Apples*, WT/DS245/R, adopted 10 December 2003, upheld by Appellate Body Report WT/DS245/AB/R, DSR 2003:IX, 4481.

———. 2010. Appellate Body Report, *China – Measures Affecting Trading Rights and Distribution Services for Certain Publications and Audiovisual Entertainment Products.* WT/DS363/AB/R, adopted 19 January 2010, para. 305–10.

———. 2012. *Beyond Tariffs: NTMs and Services Measures in the 21st Century.* Geneva: WTO.

CHAPTER 2

Streamlining NTMs: The Issues

This chapter considers the policy process of simplifying and improving trade-related regulations. The message is that this process should be analytically sound and balanced: On one hand, it should question the rationale for government intervention, its targeting, and its efficacy and not take the legitimacy of government intervention for granted. On the other hand, it should consider broad social objectives, including the preservation of local public goods—consumer safety, environment conservation, and the like—and not take the reduction of business costs as the unique, overarching objective of regulatory improvement. The chapter provides practical guidance on how to conduct this delicate balancing act.

Justifying the existence of a non-tariff measure (NTM), like any regulation—or making a case for its change or elimination—requires a comparison of outcomes with and without the measure according to some criterion ultimately related to the home country's welfare. The basic problem is that only one circumstance—the world either with or without the NTM—can be observed. In a regulatory impact assessment (RIA), the assessment is carried out ex ante, before the measure is put in place; so the scenario without the NTM is the observed one, while the scenario with it can only be "guessed" or simulated. By contrast, in an ex-post review, the scenario with the NTM is the observed one, while the scenario without exists only in memory.

Thus, the informational problem encountered in an NTM review is opposite of that of an RIA. Because of this difference, the appropriate techniques for the comparison of outcomes with and without regulation are different. In the case of an RIA, the appropriate techniques rely on ex-ante model-based simulations.[1] In the case of a review, the appropriate techniques rely on ex-post econometrics-based comparisons of outcomes, using outside references—for example, countries without the regulation—as proxies for the scenario without the NTM. This chapter will clarify the conceptual and empirical issues involved in the second exercise.

Before discussing the available techniques for an NTM review, two important caveats must be stated. First, when an economy is riddled with "distortions"—government measures and situations that work against social welfare, such as trade barriers and domestic market power, or multiple loopholes in enforcement—it is possible that eliminating one of those distortions but not others might paradoxically make things worse, not better. This is the time-honored "Theorem of the Second Best." For instance, Datt and Yang (2011) show that when the Philippine government decided to close a tariff-evasion loophole by reducing the threshold for mandatory inspection, importers switched to the Export Processing Zone, another loophole. As a result, closing the first loophole failed to raise additional revenue, while using the Export Processing Zone involved wasteful costs for importers. In the end, everyone was worse off. Keeping effects of this type in mind, the analyst should very carefully identify ways in which reforming one regulation could have perverse effects on the behavior of economic operators in the presence of other sub-optimal regulations or institutional arrangements. A careful review of one NTM may involve suggesting broader changes in the architecture of import and business regulations. Even if those interactions and how to deal with them go beyond the mandate of the NTM review body, they should be flagged in its final report and recommendations.

Second, this chapter will assume that NTMs were always put in place by benevolent governments in order to maximize social welfare, and bad regulations were only the result of mistakes. In reality, voluminous economics literature shows that governments do not maximize welfare. Politicians are rational economic actors who maximize their probability of reelection or the rents they extract while in power. This maximizing act implies placating special interests, sparing others, or even, in extreme cases, creating deliberate obstacles in order to extract side payments or campaign contributions in return for exemptions. Even in the absence of hidden agendas, the behavior of government agencies and ministries often reflects a strict, sometimes legalistic, interpretation of their mandate, with little regard for cross-agency or cross-ministry issues. For instance, the proliferation of permits and licenses may simply reflect the fact that each ministry wants to ensure that the restrictions that fall under its mandate are respected, irrespective of what other ministries do. Understanding these motivations and how they may have distorted the initial design of an NTM under review may enable the analyst to get a quicker and better grasp of what went wrong, what needs to be fixed, and what can realistically be fixed.

Third, as triggers for the review of an NTM are likely to come from sectors that feel harmed by it (potential winners from change), it is crucial for the analyst to get an equally clear idea of who are its beneficiaries (potential losers from change), even though they may not have manifested themselves at the trigger point. First, it may be the case that producers claiming to be hurt by a regulation, possibly represented by an industry association, portray themselves as representative of the whole industry, even though they represent only a segment of it—say, large producers—and changing the regulation would have large distributional effects within the industry. Second, identifying potential losers that might result from the change may help the analyst to think of compensation mechanisms to make the change acceptable. Such compensation mechanisms may not themselves be trade-related measures. For instance, suppose that a restrictive licensing scheme makes it difficult to import a product that competes with domestic production. By facilitating imports, the licensing scheme's elimination will likely lead to a drop in the domestic price, hurting domestic producers. The government may then consider other measures in areas such as public services, non-trade regulations, or the like that would simultaneously reduce the cost of doing business for the affected producers. The NTM review body is only mandated to propose the elimination of the NTM if its costs outweigh its benefits, not to propose such compensations. However, it may be best placed to think about them in the course of the discussions surrounding the regulatory review body's report.

The political-economy considerations briefly mentioned are important for the ultimate feasibility of reform when it is necessary. However, they should never induce self-censoring of the NTM review body, which should lay out the facts and arguments in an objective, transparent, and matter-of-fact manner. The working hypothesis of this toolkit and of the

World Bank's approach to NTM streamlining is that, except in environments where policy capture by special interests is extreme, there is substantial scope for substituting analysis and fact-finding for confrontation in the discussion of trade regulations. Experience on the ground suggests that government agencies and ministries typically have partial and self-centered views of policies that fall under their purview even when those policies have spillovers in other areas. The essence of the toolkit is to trigger a debate about all aspects of trade measures in which everyone is exposed to everything, so there can be a balanced debate about overall costs and benefits. The menu of institutional setups laid out in chapter 3 is meant to create conditions for that debate to take place in the best of conditions. Based on these premises, the rest of this chapter will be confined to discussion of *non-political* welfare considerations.

Beginning the NTM Review

The NTM review analyzed here proceeds in four broad steps. The review starts with input from stakeholders suggesting change: private operators who encounter compliance costs, nongovernmental organizations or consumer associations that question the NTM's efficacy, or government agencies other than the one enforcing the NTM. Complainants will typically be a precious source of information and, since they have a vested interest in the review, will be forthcoming in providing information. The information, of course, will have to be carefully verified. If preliminary information suggests a genuine case for review, the analyst can proceed to stage two. Appendix B includes a questionnaire that could help assess the substance of the complaints and determine whether a review process should be initiated.

In stage two, the analyst needs to seek input from the agency enforcing the NTM, using the assessment guidelines provided in appendix C. The assessment guidelines are specific to broad families of measures, with SPS/TBT technical regulation vs. quantitative restriction, the most frequently encountered. The assessment guidelines have been tested in the field and are designed to elicit and organize key information for the review, following the analytical structure laid out in this section. Responses to the questionnaire from the enforcement agency can be completed, after the interview, with information from other sources so as to lead to a coherent body of information on each issue.

In stage three, the analyst builds on the information gathered in interviews to build the formal analysis. This will, in all likelihood, involve more fact-finding, going back to stakeholders for more precise figures, and verifying information. After a number of rounds, the range of estimates on key parameters typically will narrow down and the analyst will get an increasingly clear picture of the stakes. If the numbers are precise, it may be possible to conduct a rough-and-ready cost-benefit analysis with a limited objective—namely, to check if the picture is completely lopsided, that is, the NTM's costs outweighing its benefits by a very wide margin, or vice versa. Finally in stage four, the analyst comes to a recommendation grounded in the analysis, or, alternatively, states the issues at stake clearly and puts them on the table in order to trigger an objective, evidence-based debate.

Reassessing the Benefits of Government Intervention

Before making a case for the elimination or modification of an existing government regulation—or for doing nothing, for that matter—the analyst should try to get a deep understanding of the regulation's justification. Conceptually, this involves first determining whether a "market failure" has occurred (see figure 2.1).

A market failure is a situation whose outcome is sub-optimal from a collective point of view, that is, where the pursuit of individual interests does not lead to the common good. For instance, suppliers of low-quality products or services may be creating so much uncertainty in the market that high-quality suppliers are driven out, a problem known as a "market for lemons." In addition, for a market failure to justify government intervention, a case must be made that market forces left to themselves will not lead to a solution; that is, in the lemons example, it must be the case that no business-to-business arrangements such as warrantees or long-term contracts can alleviate the problem.

Market failures essentially involve situations which, in economic jargon, are characterized by "imperfect information," or by production or consumption "externalities" (or public goods—the two concepts are related).[2] In a trade context, market failures can involve cases where consumers are insufficiently informed and may harm themselves or others by purchasing defective imported products, cases where the import or export of certain products creates a hazard for biodiversity or the environment, or cases where non-compatibility between products of different origins makes them useless.

For instance, imported medications may be manufactured in a country with loose production controls, resulting in highly uneven quality and

Figure 2.1 Flowchart of an NTM Review

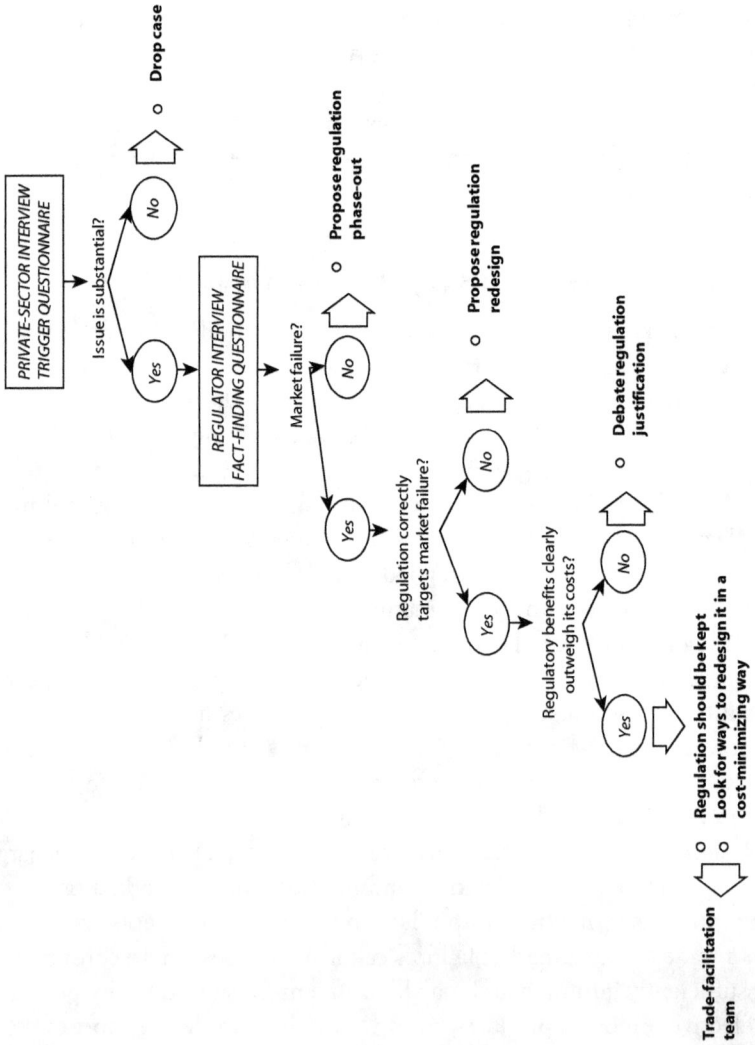

PRIVATE-SECTOR INTERVIEW
TRIGGER QUESTIONNAIRE

Issue is substantial?

Yes   No

o **Drop case**

REGULATOR INTERVIEW
FACT-FINDING QUESTIONNAIRE

Market failure?

Yes   No

o **Propose regulation
phase-out**

Regulation correctly
targets market failure?

Yes   No

o **Propose regulation
redesign**

Regulatory benefits clearly
outweigh its costs?

Yes   No

o **Debate regulation
justification**

**Trade-facilitation
team**

o **Regulation should be kept**
o **Look for ways to redesign it in a
cost-minimizing way**

products that are ineffective or harmful. The market failure (imperfect information) comes from the fact that testing medications for safety is too costly to be undertaken by individual buyers. It can be further characterized in terms of either "moral hazard" (a term borrowed from the jargon of insurance), or "adverse selection." In general, moral hazard comprises hidden behavior by a party to a transaction that reduces the value of that transaction to the other party. Here, foreign producers deliberately under-invest in quality, hoping that buyers will not notice or will notice too late. Adverse selection is usually a situation wherein choices made by one party to a transaction lead him/her to do business with just the bad counterparts he would like to avoid. For instance, selecting the lowest bidder in a tender may return the worst suppliers. Or, for a bank, charging a high interest rate may attract only the riskiest borrowers. In a trade context, it means that, for want of rules or standards, the home country's supply chains attract the worst suppliers.

Can market forces take care of this problem? Whether it is moral hazard or adverse selection, the general answer is yes. Market forces can be expected to lead to the emergence of arrangements, contractual or other, that alleviate the problem. For instance, good suppliers may signal their quality by offering warrantees. Wholesale buyers may screen suppliers for quality (what individual buyers cannot afford) and offer long-term contracts to good ones. So the baseline scenario is unlikely to be one where the market failure persists indefinitely. However, the next question is, how long is it going to take before either producers get their act together, or intermediaries do their job? It may well be that those things will ultimately happen, but too slowly to make the baseline scenario acceptable. In that case, home government action is legitimate.

Alternatively, hazards may come from imported plants and animals carrying invasive organisms that threaten biodiversity, or the export of rare species or over-exploitation of natural resources can deplete or harm the environment. Here the market failure does not come from imperfect information, but from externalities or public goods. If agents could agree not to import harmful products or not to export irreplaceable resources, there would be no problem. But an individual agent is unlikely to recognize that even though he is too small to affect the environment, if everyone acts like him, the outcome will be detrimental for society at large. Likewise, producers may fail to take the (costly) steps necessary to coordinate with competitors on a common technical standard at the time of product development, leading to unnecessary fragmentation.

Again, can market forces take care of the problem? Coordination problems are sometimes overcome by collective action among private-sector actors, but often they are not. For instance, responsible environmental management is encouraged by private labeling schemes, but cooperative arrangements are liable to free-riding and ultimate unraveling unless they are accompanied by sanctions in case of breach, which are difficult to enforce without a legal framework. In such situations, government intervention may prove necessary to overcome private interests. The government can indeed be viewed as having as its fundamental mission the expression of a collective will that transcends private interests.

Precisely Locating the Focus of Regulatory Intervention

After establishing the legitimacy of regulatory action, the next task is to locate precisely where the market failure lies in order to better target the intervention. The notion that regulatory or other policy interventions should be targeted as closely as possible to the source of the problem is known as the "targeting principle."[3] For instance, if society wants to shelter workers from severe income loss in case of unemployment (a problem located in the labor market), it is more efficient to offer unemployment benefits (an intervention targeting the labor market) than to protect domestic industries with tariffs or non-tariff measures (interventions targeting product markets).

Whether a market failure is due to imperfect information or to an externality, the first issue to sort out is its location, that is, whether it is associated with the *use* of a particular good or with its *production*. If the problem is generated by a production activity, it is essentially a domestic regulatory issue. As defined by the Multi-Agency Support Team (MAST) classification, NTMs do not include instruments that regulate domestic production activities, so even though production regulations may well affect the international competitiveness of domestic firms, this issue will not be considered for now. If, by contrast, the problem is linked to the use of a particular product—whether as an intermediate input or as a final consumption good—NTMs may be used in as much as the product is not only produced domestically but also imported.

What does it mean in practical terms to target an NTM as close as possible to the source of the market failure? Think of a value chain in which an imported toxic chemical is used in the domestic production of a final good for consumption. Suppose first that the chemical's toxicity disappears in the process of transformation into a final good and does generate toxic effluents out of the factory. In that case, final consumers never get in direct contact with the chemical, so all the government needs to worry about is whether it creates a hazard for workers in the production process. The government may then consider either banning its sale—an NTM—or regulating production by mandating processes that do not use it or protect workers—not an NTM if the technical regulation mandates a process without reference to a product. Suppose now, on the contrary, that the chemical's toxicity creates a hazard for consumers once embodied in the final consumption good. Then the government may consider regulating the chemical content of the "final good" when sold on the domestic market, because that is where the problem is, irrespective of its origin (domestically produced or imported). Regulating only the *import* of the final product would be discriminatory, and regulating only the import of the *intermediate* would open a loophole by allowing imports of final goods containing the chemical.

Quantifying the Cost of a Market Failure

Many NTMs, in particular technical standards, are put in place to protect public health, and methods to evaluate the market failures they address have been developed in the health-economics literature (see Hammit 2002 and the very complete analytical survey in van Tongeren, Beghin, and Marette 2009). One family of methods relies on the notion of QALY (quality-adjusted life years) which measures health hazards in two dimensions, mortality (life expectancy) and morbidity (quality of life, that is, health measured in a continuous way as opposed to mortality, which is binary). One advantage of QALY methods is that they do not require individuals to know what hazards they are exposed to, since risks are measured independently. In some cases, changes in mortality are weighted by the income of the individuals affected in order to aggregate them into changes in overall wealth creation (Freeman 1993).

When individuals are aware of the externalities they are exposed to, alternative methods can be used relying on the concept of Willingness To Pay (WTP), which is simply how much individuals are willing to pay to avoid being exposed to a "bad"—hazard, externality, or poor-quality product or service. The WTP approach makes it possible to include in the analysis the disutility of being exposed to the bad rather than just the effect on health and productivity. WTP estimates can be obtained as part of laboratory and field experiments,[4] and the recent explosion of "experimental economics" provides many examples and methods (see, for example, van Tongeren, Beghin, and Marette 2009 and references therein). Many WTP experiments, surveyed in Costa-Font, Gil, and

Traill (2008), have been conducted to elicit the disutility associated with consuming genetically modified organisms, sometimes with surprising results (for instance, French consumers were shown in Noussair, Robin, and Ruffieux [2002] to be relatively indifferent to the issue, in contrast to the extensive media coverage and strict regulatory treatment of genetically modified organisms in the European Union). Willingness to pay for biodiversity has been explored through the auction of "conservation contracts" (see Latacz-Lohman and Schilizzi 2005 for a survey; see also Stoneham, Chaudry, and Strappazzon 2003 for an application).

Useful information to cost production SPS externalities can be found in the Centre for Agriculture and Biosciences International (CABI) Crop Protection Compendium[5] and in the surveys of Pimentel, Zuniga, and Morrison (2000) and Pimental et al. (2005) who provide estimates of the costs of various pests for U.S. agriculture. Overall estimates of those losses vary over a wide range, $4.7 billion and $136 billion per year. Models of pest infestation dynamics (spatial or other) can be found in recent papers surveyed in van Tongeren, Beghin, and Marette (2009). Costello et al. (2007) show that the risk of alien pest invasion varies across trading partners and increases with trade volumes, although at a decreasing rate. A crude cost-benefit exercise also suggests that quantitative restrictions on imports to control pest invasions would cost the economy more than the expected cost savings on pest invasions.

Reassessing the Costs of Government Intervention

As discussed at the beginning of this chapter, unlike a regulatory impact assessment, an ex-post review can rely on existing data to assess, using econometric or other techniques, the effect of an NTM by comparing outcomes observed in its presence with outcomes observed in its absence in comparable settings. This section will briefly review available quantitative tools for this comparison exercise, but first it is important to clarify what type of costs are to be considered.

The Australian Government Office of Best Practice Regulation offers an online tool, the Business Cost Calculator (BCC), designed to help businesses calculate their regulatory compliance costs. The BCC's cost categories are listed in table 2.1, adapted from Australia (2010). Although the BCC categories are listed without hierarchy, in the case of NTMs, some of its categories stand out as more important than others. For instance, "purchase costs" are of critical importance in the case of NTMs, whereas

Table 2.1   BCC Categories of Compliance Costs

Compliance tasks	Example
Notification	Advance notification for import of foodstuffs or medications
Education	Watch for new regulatory requirements
Permission	Cost of acquiring import licenses
Purchase cost	Higher price of imported inputs that comply with technical regulations
Record keeping	Cost of recording detailed information on inputs to comply with technical regulations or rules of origin
Enforcement	Cost incurred as part of inspections and audits
Publication & documentation	Cost of labeling and marking
Procedures	Cost of reorganizing production to obtain certification of production sites
Other	

Source: Adapted from Australia (2010), table G1.

"education" may not stand out. For this discussion, the BCC categories will be organized in two **broad classes:**

- **Sourcing costs**, embodying "Purchase cost" and "Procedures," which are reflected in the higher price of imported products affected by an NTM, and
- **Verification costs**, embodying all other categories, which are reflected in paperwork and managerial costs for importers.

The next two sections review methods for calculating these costs, first pointing out one issue the analyst must watch out for. Compliance costs, whether linked to sourcing or to enforcement, are rarely distributed evenly among private-sector operators. For instance, big players will face different costs than smaller ones, but will portray their complaints as if they applied to all operators alike. Seeking out opinions from the private sector should involve some (informal) sampling to ensure results are representative. For instance, when private-sector representatives like a chamber of commerce or industry association claims that there has been exit from the industry as a result of government regulation, it may be instructive to talk to some of the operators who did exit to check if they did so because of the regulation or for other reasons. The bottom line of such discussions essentially will be whether the country had or has a comparative advantage in the sector claiming injury from regulation. In some cases, the analyst will discover that the firms claiming injury from the government were caught competing in the wrong segment of the market where fierce price competition from foreign competitors gave them no chance anyway.

Assessing the Sourcing Costs of NTMs

This section provides a guide on how to assess the cost-raising effect of NTMs through induced changes in sourcing, excluding the paperwork and verification costs. That is, suppose a regulation mandates that vegetables sold on the domestic market must contain no more than a given residual level of pesticides. Vegetables will now have to be sourced from producers who comply with the regulation, implying either changes in the traditional suppliers' production methods or a switch to alternative ones. In either case, supply prices are likely to go up. How can we estimate by how much they will rise?

Price-Gap Analysis

The primary tool for assessing the trade effects of NTMs is price-gap analysis, recommended for the calculation of ad-valorem equivalents (AVEs) of NTMs in agriculture by Annex V of the WTO Agriculture Agreement.[6] Price-gap analysis establishes the price effect of an NTM, providing a preliminary step to welfare analysis. Higher prices on the domestic market mean both lower consumer surplus, which reduces welfare, and higher producer surplus, which raises it. In the case of NTMs, there is no tariff revenue, so the net effect on welfare is the sum of the changes in consumer and producer surplus.

Price-gap analysis is a fairly straightforward method that requires no particular knowledge of econometrics. To understand the method, suppose that the home country imposes a non-automatic licensing system for the import of widgets. Widgets are expensive to produce on the home market because they require skills that are in short supply in the domestic labor market. As a result, the supply of widgets is restricted, pushing their price up. The aim here is to measure the price increase that is attributable to the licensing system.

The analysis relies on a comparison of the price of widgets on the home market, where the NTM under scrutiny is applied, and a comparator market, where it is not. The comparator market should be similar to the domestic market in at least some of the following dimensions:

- Size, so there is no large difference in the ability of distributors to reap economies of scale;

- Income level, so quality and market positioning are comparable; and
- Remoteness (distance to main economic centers), so transportation costs are comparable.

In practice, it is rare that a comparator market is similar in all these dimensions, so in most cases there will be systematic cost-of-living (COL) differences between the home and the comparator markets, which must be controlled for. Thus, the analysis proceeds in two steps.

Step 1 (COL Adjustment). Let $\bar{p}^H$ and $\bar{p}^C$ be the average prices, on the home and comparator markets, of a basket of commodities that are sold in both markets and have NTMs in neither. Let also $\bar{t}^H$ and $\bar{t}^C$ be their respective tariffs. The formula for the COL adjustment, derived in appendix D, is

$$\lambda = \frac{\bar{p}^H \big/ \left(1+\bar{t}^H\right)}{\bar{p}^C \big/ \left(1+\bar{t}^C\right)} - 1 \tag{1}$$

This parameter has the form of an AVE. That is, a value of λ equal to 0.12 means that the cost of living is 12 percent higher in the home country than in the comparator country, based on the basket of products used in the comparison.

Alternatively, it is possible to use an "off-the-shelf" COL adjustment using existing databases, such as the World Bank's International Price Comparison Project. Data issues will be discussed in the next section.

Step 2 (AVE Calculation). The average price of widgets on the domestic market, p^H, is compared to their price p^C in the comparator market using a formula for the COL-adjusted price gap, also derived in appendix D, yielding an estimate for a, the NTM's AVE:

$$a = \frac{p^H \big/ \left[\left(1+t^H\right)\left(1+\lambda\right)\right]}{p^C \big/ \left(1+t^C\right)} - 1 \tag{2}$$

The price-gap method requires data on prices in the NTM-ridden market and in a comparator market, which is usually difficult to find.

The first task is to identify the prices to use in the analysis, whether it is the CIF (cost, insurance, and freight) unit value of imports, wholesale prices, or retail prices. Wholesale prices are preferable to retail prices in order to filter out the effect of differences in distribution costs—although the structure of distribution channels may well be influenced by NTMs.[7] Likewise, wholesale domestic prices would be preferable for importing unit values, as those may or may not embody the AVE of NTMs, depending on the type of NTM. For instance, if licenses are distributed or sold to domestic importers, import unit values may not embody their AVE. However, wholesale prices are notoriously difficult to measure.[8] Domestic prices at the retail or wholesale level can be collected in the home country. The problem is that it is more difficult to carry out the data-collection exercise in the comparator country. The Economist Intelligence Unit (EIU) publishes retail prices for a basket of consumer products, which can also be used.[9] In their absence, import unit values are an acceptable fallback.

As for the COL adjustment, one useful source—as an alternative to the ad-hoc calculation of λ as detailed in the previous section—is to use the World Bank International Comparison Program (ICP). The ICP publishes comparative price, expenditure, and purchasing power parity data for 200 countries in 2005 (only one year is currently available). Price data show each country's average domestic price compared to the average world price (fixed at 100) for products (including food and non-alcoholic beverages, alcoholic beverages and tobacco, clothing and footwear, furnishings and household equipment, and machinery and equipment), as well as services (for example, housing and utilities, health, transport, communication and culture, education, restaurants and hotels, and construction), as well as a number of ad-hoc aggregates, including GDP and individual consumption.[10] The main quality of these price comparisons is that they result from extremely careful data collection and processing. The main drawback is that they are fairly aggregated, and thus not suitable to track the effect of a single NTM defined at the tariff-line levels. However, it can be argued that what matters is the overall effect of an NTM on household budgets: if it is too narrowly applied to have any traceable effect, then perhaps the thorough review implied by a price-gap exercise is unnecessary.

ICP data should be used for COL adjustment. The comparison of Indonesian and Philippine prices in table 2.2 shows that, overall, the price levels are very similar (the percentage difference between the two at the broadest GDP level is 2.65 percent); large individual differences persist for services (for example, education, –21.95 percent, communication, 13.61 percent, or recreation and culture, –12.9 percent), but for merchandise, the only large differences are for alcoholic beverages and tobacco (135 percent) and clothing and footwear (–22.06). These differences are likely to be due to policy interventions. Thus, if one were to take the

Table 2.2   Average Domestic Price Indices by Category (world average = 100), Indonesia and the Philippines

Code	Aggregate (product category)	Indonesia	Philippines	% difference
1	GDP	50.299	49.001	2.65
11	Actual individual consumption	45.919	46.787	−1.86
1101	Food and non-alcoholic beverages	66.905	68.086	−1.74
1102	Alcoholic beverages and tobacco	82.553	35.106	135.15
1103	Clothing and footwear	41.108	52.743	−22.06
1104	Housing, water, electricity, gas, and other fuels	54.777	52.437	4.46
1105	Furnishings, household equipment and household maintenance	47.678	48.282	−1.25
1106	Health	34.195	30.830	10.91
1107	Transport	54.802	55.321	−0.94
1108	Communication	91.013	80.110	13.61
1109	Recreation and culture	42.710	49.037	−12.90
1110	Education	18.336	23.491	−21.95
1111	Restaurants and hotels	45.451	48.697	−6.67
1112	Miscellaneous goods and services	40.351	43.946	−8.18
1113	Net purchases from abroad			
11A	Individual consumption expenditure by households	49.391	50.180	−1.57
11B	Individual consumption expenditure by government	26.405	28.539	−7.48
14	Collective consumption expenditure by government	42.466	38.392	10.61
15	Gross fixed capital formation	59.230	52.845	12.08
1501	Machinery and equipment	101.847	93.341	9.11
1502	Construction	43.796	37.627	16.39
1503	Other products	59.595	53.116	12.20

Source: International Comparison Project database. Codes are ICP codes. Each price is in percent of the average world price for that category in the database. The last column is the percentage difference between the first two.

Philippines as comparator for Indonesia in the context of an NTM review, no overall COL adjustment would be called for.

Off-the-Shelf AVE Estimates

An alternative method for assessing trade effects of NTMs is to use "off-the-shelf" estimates of the ad-valorem equivalent of NTMs, obtained from cross-country econometric studies (see Ferrantino 2006 for a sample survey). Using such estimates has the advantage of convenience, since the hard work of deriving them has already been done. However, this method has two drawbacks compared to the price-gap method. First, typically, these estimates bundle NTMs into fairly broad aggregates, masking potentially important differences between measures. Second, they estimate *average* effects of NTMs across the sample of countries used for the estimation. Thus, if one country applies a given NTM in a harsher way than another, the estimates will not be able to pick up that difference in application.

One prominent method, developed by Hiau Looi Kee, Alessandro Nicita, and Marcelo Olarreaga at the World Bank, relies on the econometric estimation of AVEs using trade-flow data rather than price data (Kee, Nicita, and Olarreaga 2009). The method consists of correlating cross-country differences in import volumes, product by product, with tariffs, the presence of NTMs, and other determinants of imports including comparative-advantage factors. The World Bank is currently working on an update of their estimates using recent data and more detailed NTM decompositions.

Reassessing the Verification Costs of NTMs

The mainstream method to assess verification costs, pioneered by the Dutch Government, is known as the Standard Cost Model and widely used in OECD countries. It consists of collecting from producers' estimates of (1) the number and position of employees routinely involved in NTM-related paperwork and (2) their average salary, then calculating an estimate of the clerk and managerial cost involved in compliance-related paperwork.

When original analysis is not feasible, information on potential effects of an NTM can sometimes be gathered from the literature if similar measures have been adopted abroad. For instance, the EU regulation on aflatoxins was shown (see Otsuki, Wilson, and Sewadeh 2001) to have a very small effect on public health, the desired effect, at a high cost to African exports of dried fruits and nuts, a negative outside spillover on market access. Adopting a similar regulation elsewhere could be expected a priori to also have a small effect on public health, although the effect on market access would depend on the size of the country adopting it.

Balancing Costs and Benefits

In the area of NTMs, like in others, the challenge of cost-benefit analysis is two-fold: (1) find a *common* metric to measure costs and benefits, which are typically very different things (like immediate business costs vs. long-term societal risks) in a comparable way, and (2) come up with estimates of those costs and benefits in the common metric.

Trade economists have recently developed integrated approaches to evaluate simultaneously the non-trade benefits and the trade costs of a regulation (see Beghin et al. 2011; Disdier and Marette 2009, 2010; van Tongeren, Beghin, and Marette 2009; Marette et al. 2008). Whereas similar methods have long been used in other areas of economics, their application to NTMs is new. This section gives a very brief introduction to them, closely following Beghin et al. (2011).

Cost-Benefit Analysis: A Brief Overview

A detailed exposition of the application of cost-benefit analysis can be found in van Tongeren, Beghin, and Marette (2009) in a partial-equilibrium framework, that is, one in which only direct effects are taken into account, to the exclusion of spillovers across markets (for instance, to labor markets). The authors propose a useful taxonomy of measures based on the type of instrument (prohibition or labeling requirement) and on the location of the market failure (consumption or production). Essentially, they propose a step-by step identification of the costs and benefits of a regulation (relative to a scenario where a market failure is left unchecked) on domestic producers, domestic consumers, and the government. Effects on foreign producers are left out of the analysis, in accordance with the general approach of this toolkit whereby NTM streamlining is considered from a domestic regulatory-improvement point of view as opposed to an international exchange-of-concessions point of view.

In order to grasp the issues, consider a technical regulation banning the importation of farmed shrimp when antibiotics have been used in their production. Antibiotics use is potentially harmful to both human health and the environment because it can encourage the development of antibiotics-resistant bacteria. The problem results from lack of coordination among exporters—they could all decide to contribute to a global public good (better health), but individually they do not have an incentive to do so. This is a case of "coordination failure" compounded by imperfect information, because it is too expensive, even for a health-conscious consumer, to verify if antibiotics were used in the production of shrimp sold in the local supermarket. In the long run, high-quality producers may be expected to adopt voluntary standards and labeling schemes like organic certification, but this may take time. Currently, organic shrimp accounts for less than 1 percent of world production (Disdier and Marette 2010).

Suppose that the government decides to address this market failure either through a labeling scheme or by mandating antibiotic-free production for shrimp sold on the domestic market, through a technical regulation.[11] The technical regulation raises production costs, as organic production requires more space (in order to reduce contact between animals) and more labor. Thus, it involves a trade-off between higher prices and public health. For simplicity, assume that there is no domestic production to compete with.

The trade-off is illustrated in figure 2.2. The downward-sloping line shows the domestic demand for imported shrimp. The lower flat line (DC) gives the CIF price of standard shrimp produced with antibiotics, while the upper one (AB) gives the CIF price of antibiotics-free (organic) shrimp. The difference, c, is the regulation's compliance cost, which is

Figure 2.2   Costs and Benefits of a Technical Regulation: The Case of Organic Shrimp

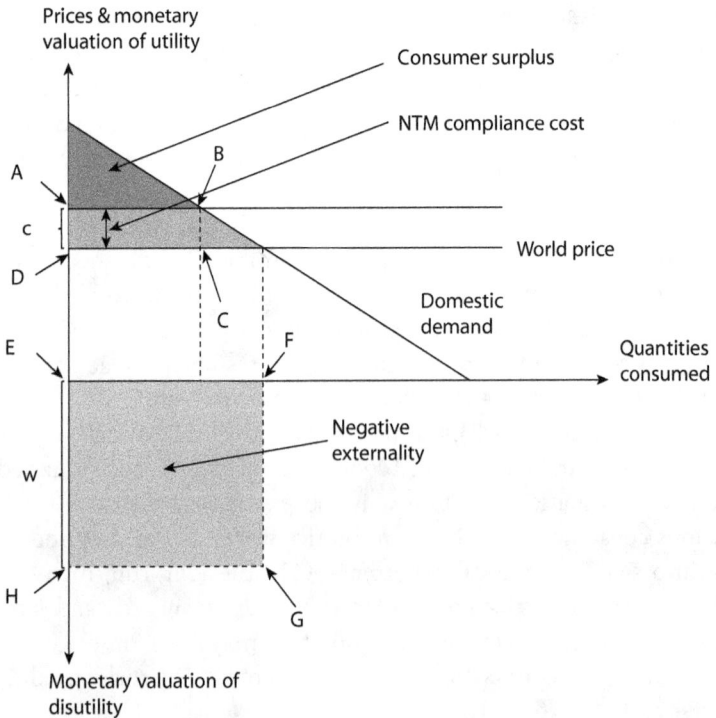

one of the two critical parameters to be estimated.[12] The grey area ABCD is the regulation's cost.

The lower rectangle EFGH is the monetary equivalent of the hazard created by the production of shrimp treated with antibiotics. It is the product of the quantity imported multiplied by a per-unit amount, w, which can be thought of as the "cost of ignorance." The regulation has eliminated this rectangle altogether, so the cost-benefit analysis consists of comparing area ABCD with area EFGH.

The key challenge is to find plausible values for w (the societal loss generated by the market failure) and c (the compliance cost). As for w, Disdier and Marette (2010) propose a direct calculation method. They ran an experiment with 160 volunteers, providing an explanation on the hazards related to the use of antibiotics in shrimp aquaculture and asking people how much they were willing to pay for a bag of standard shrimp (1) without the information, (2) with the information. The difference between the two is the cost of ignorance. The result was that the willingness to pay went down from €2.14 to €1.13, or a decrease of 47 percent. This provides an estimate of w. Alternatively, in the case of health hazards, it may be necessary to estimate costs and risks directly. For instance, estimate the decrease in mortality attributable to a regulation and combine it with a "price of life" inferred from individual attitudes toward risk.[13]

As for c, Disdier and Marette (2010) used the simple method of asking producers for an estimate of the compliance cost. In the case of shrimp farming, upgrading to organic production was estimated to raise the cost of a bag from €5.00 to €8.00, a compliance cost of €3.00, or 60 percent. Suppose that this is the price increase generated by the measure. We now want to go from price increase to welfare effect. In partial-equilibrium analysis, this involves a formula, derived in the appendix, of the form

$$\Delta W = E_0 a \left(1 - \frac{\varepsilon a}{2} \right) \tag{3}$$

where a is the AVE estimated by the methods outline above and ε is the price elasticity of demand (in algebraic form, that is, negative).

Using estimated elasticities in a similar partial-equilibrium framework, Disdier and Marette find a welfare gain of €1.398 million from the elimination of the market failure (area EFGH) against a consumer-surplus loss of €756,000 (area ABCD). Thus, in this exercise, even though the AVE of the NTM is a whopping 60 percent, the welfare calculation returns a welfare *gain*.

This simple exercise can be easily complicated by adding domestic producers and other refinements. The point here is to illustrate the general procedure and also to highlight the fact that trade costs alone can be a very misleading guide as to which are "good" vs. "bad" NTMs.

Horizons and Timing: Discounting

Future costs and benefits must be "discounted" to be comparable with present ones. If costs and benefits all accrue at the same pace, the choice of a discount rate is inconsequential. However, if costs are incurred today (say, searching for a different supplier or providing technical assistance to overseas producers to help them get in compliance) and benefits, in the form of reduced risks, accrue every year at a constant pace, then the discount rate matters. A high discount rate will reduce the present discounted value of the benefits and therefore make the cost-benefit analysis of the NTM less favorable. Also, at a high discount rate, giving firms a grace period to comply will reduce the net present value (NPV) of the compliance costs substantially.

To see why discount rates so affect the NPV, compare a one-time, sunk cost of compliance with a technical regulation equal to, say, $100,000 today. A firm given a grace period of 10 years to comply could set aside today the required amount and invest it on the stock market. Suppose that the rate of return on the stock market is 5 percent per year on average. Then the firm can set aside an amount x which, if reinvested every year, will become, after 10 years, $X = x (1.05)^9 = 1.55x$. For that amount to be equal to $100,000, the firm has to set aside only $100,000/1.55 = $64,461. Thus, a dollar in 10 years, at a 5 percent discount rate, is worth only $0.64 today. Suppose now that the return on the stock market is 10 percent. Then the same calculation gives $X = 2.357x$, so the firm would have to set aside only $100,000/2.357 = $42,409. Thus, with a 10 percent discount rate, the grace period allows the firm to set aside a smaller amount. Note that all future values can be evaluated in "real" (inflation-adjusted) terms, so the rate of inflation can be ignored.

"Real Options" and the Cost of Irreversible Decisions

The issue of irreversibility is potentially important in the case of SPS and other regulations, which may be meant to protect the environment from invasive species or plant and animal diseases. Some diseases are characterized by only temporary outbreaks; others, however, spread to the environment in a way that cannot be controlled and they remain, having potentially permanent effects on biodiversity. Similarly, when a species is driven to extinction, it may not be possible to reintroduce it later on. The effect is then irreversible.

Treating reversible and irreversible options the same way in a cost-benefit analysis would lead to severely distorted decisions, as was shown long ago in the literature.[14] The intuition is as follows: Suppose that a regulation is in place to prohibit the import of a certain vegetable species that can carry micro-organisms that would spread irreversibly in the environment and generate damage. The private sector is claiming that this prohibition is hurting business and asks for its elimination. If the government eliminates the regulation today, it cannot reverse its act tomorrow—the microorganism is in the environment and cannot be recalled. However, if it maintains the regulation, it keeps the option of eliminating it next year or any time later on. For the government, it is as if it was holding an option on an asset. If the value of the asset goes up—that is, if the regulation's cost to business escalates—it can exercise the option. If it goes down—that is, if the regulation's cost to business goes down—it can hold on to it. The value of this option can be calculated using option-pricing techniques. Ignoring it would bias the calculation, and in the case of irreversible decisions with potentially large consequences, the bias can be very large.

Even when one option is not strictly irreversible, but entails reversion costs—say, the cost of cleaning up after a large polluting event—the reasoning remains largely the same. That is, treating an option that entails reversion costs as if it was fully reversible would bias the cost-benefit analysis. The case of partial reversibility, which is equivalent to sunk costs of entry and/or exit, is treated formally in appendix D.

Chapter 5 details three case studies illustrating the techniques and approaches discussed here. Note that proper cost-benefit analysis entails, in particular for SPS measures, an expert analysis of the non-trade aspects of the measure and its potential change. This goes beyond the purpose of this toolkit, but should be included in the review measure to properly inform policy makers on all aspects of the regulation. It is also worth noting that a government may achieve the intended policy objectives by adopting risk management and a risk-based approach to control imports rather than implementing overly trade restrictive NTMs. This topic also goes beyond the scope of this toolkit. Box 2.1 presents the key concepts. The issue is also largely addressed in other publications including in McLinden et al. (2011) which provides extensive information on a broad range of international developments and contemporary principles applicable to all aspects of border management, irrespective of which agency is in charge.

Box 2.1

NTMs and the Case for Risk Management in Border Agencies

The practice of most governments is to assign aspects of regulatory responsibility at the border to a number of different agencies. Each of these agencies has its own specific mandate from government, and taken together they cover issues as diverse as health, product safety, biosecurity, immigration controls, revenue collection, and transport security. Nevertheless, the fundamental nature of the challenge that each agency confronts is the same, that is, to facilitate the legitimate movement of people and goods, while at the same time maintaining the integrity of the border by ensuring compliance with relevant legal requirements.

Proper border management is critical to the cost-effectiveness of international trade transactions and the smooth flow of legitimate goods and people from the perspective of both the public and private sector. And while some agencies may have particularly good procedures in place, the achievement of effective and efficient border management is ultimately a whole-of-government task, requiring the involvement of all government agencies with responsibilities at the border. This also highlights the need to regulate borders in a way that reduces the impact of interventionist strategies as much as possible. In other words, while maintaining cross border control is nonnegotiable, the way in which it is achieved should also provide appropriate levels of facilitation.

Risk management can help SPS and TBT administrations to handle this trade-off by focusing attention and resources on the riskiest transactions. This is particularly crucial as SPS and TBT administrations are often impotent to efficiently enforce and control the declarations and shipments' compliance. Often lacking modern technologies, they also suffer from a lack of coordination with more modern Custom's administrations. As SPS agencies are much smaller and far less modernized than Customs agencies, notably regarding information technology infrastructure, capacity building should be expected from Custom's to SPS agencies, especially given that much of the data that are required to implement risk-based analysis for technical measures are already part of custom's management system.

Finally, it is difficult and counter-productive for the administration to control and check every transaction. With limited resources, opportunity costs of inspecting both low-risk and high-risk importers are high: while wasting time and spending mostly on compliant importers, resources dedicated to high-risk importers are reduced. A risk-based approach contributes to reverting this situation toward

(continued next page)

Box 2.1   *(continued)*

a win-win situation. It defines the actions (sample tests, full inspection etc.) to associate to each transaction depending on its risk profile, which itself results from the assessment of the declaration's risk of infraction. The latter relies on historical data of the transaction's characteristics, in other words whether or not the elements of the declarations have previously been associated to fraudulent declarations. By providing appropriate prioritization of actions through the targeting of the riskiest transactions, risk-based processes enable more efficient resources allocation.

Border agencies should integrate the concept of risk in their search for compliance with regulations. Risk has two elements: the likelihood of something happening, and the consequences if it does in fact happen. The combination of these factors provides an understanding of the overall level of risk, which then allows the administration to compare and prioritize the variety of risks that have been identified. Then the aim is to determine the relative significance of each risk to make informed decisions.

Notes

1. Model-based simulations can rely on either partial-equilibrium analysis, where markets are analyzed in isolation at a high degree of detail, or general-equilibrium analysis, where all cross-market interactions are analyzed in very complex models, albeit at the cost of a lesser degree of product-level detail.

2. A third type of market failures relate to imperfect competition (the existence and possible abuse of monopoly power), but these competition issues are outside the scope of this volume, as they are (or should be) mostly dealt with by competition policy rather than NTMs.

3. See Rodrik (1987) and references therein. The original idea was developed in the context of taxation by Pigou in the 1930s.

4. Laboratory experiments are conducted in very controlled settings such as university laboratories where volunteers are faced with sophisticated experimental choices to elicit preferences. Field experiments are conducted outside laboratories—for example, in stores—and face individuals with carefully crafted, although possibly simpler, choices in more realistic settings. See List (2006) for a discussion of the relative advantages of field experiments versus other methods.

5. The CABI compendium (www.cabi.org/cpc) is a site, maintained by the 40 partners of the International Development Consortium, containing information on more than 3,500 pests, diseases, natural enemies, and crops, with

information on more than 20,000 species and scientific findings stored in 189,000 bibliographic records.

6. See the WTO Agreement on Agriculture, http://www.wto.org/english/docs_e/legal_e/14-ag_02_e.htm#annV, for details on the calculation method.

7. For instance, non-automatic licensing may give market power to license holders; if they are also the retail distributors, retail prices will be affected by the distribution of licenses.

8. For instance, in the course of the WTO dispute on bananas, widely different estimates of the wholesale price of bananas in the EU were produced by experts and law firms supporting the various parties involved in the dispute.

9. The Economist Intelligence Unit (EIU) publishes a database of consumer prices for cost-of-living adjustment of expatriate compensation. The database (http://www.worldwidecostofliving.com/asp/wcol_WCOLHome.asp), is sold on a pay-per-view basis at a substantial price. Alternatively, the United Nations International Civil Service Commission has a COL division that maintains a site for COL adjustment calculations (http://icsc.un.org/col-par.asp). Thanks to Gianluca Mele for this information.

10. Available disaggregated data are not as disaggregated as trade data (the HS6 level has 5,000 products) and thus cannot adequately pick up the effect of an NTM applied narrowly to a product defined at the tariff-line (HS8, even finer than HS6) level. However, many NTMs are applied to product categories broader than the tariff line or even the HS6 level; in those cases, the level of disaggregation provided in the ICP data may be sufficient.

11. This is the route taken recently by the European Commission.

12. The ratio of the compliance cost c to the before-regulation world price is the regulation's ad-valorem equivalent.

13. The authoritative source on this is Viscusi (1993). One method consists of observing the wage premium (Δw) that workers require to take jobs entailing higher probabilities of fatality (Δr). Extrapolating $\Delta w/\Delta r$ gives an implicit "price of life."

14. The literature originates with Henry (1974); see Dixit and Pyndick (1994) for an exhaustive treatment.

References

Australia. 2010. *Best Practice Regulation Handbook.* Canberra: Australian Government.

Beghin, John, A.-C. Disdier, S. Marette, and F. van Tongeren. 2011. "Measuring Costs and Benefits of Non-Tariff Measures in Agri-Food Trade." Iowa State University Working Paper 11001 Ames, Iowa.

Costa-Font, Montserrat, José Gil, and W. Bruce Traill. 2008. "Consumer Acceptance, Valuation of and Attitudes Towards Genetically Modified Food: Review and Implications for Food Policy." *Food Policy* 33 (2): 99–111.

Costello, Christopher, M. Springborn, C. McAusland, and A. Solow. 2007. "Unintended Biological Invasions: Does Risk Vary by Trading Partner?" *Journal of Environmental Economics and Management* 54: 262–76.

Datt, Mohini, and D. Yang. 2011. "Caught at Customs, Running on Scylla, Wishing to Avoid Charybdis: A Natural Experiment Reveals How a Trade Policy Intervention Affects Importer Behavior." In *Where to Send the Next Million? Applying Impact Evaluation to Trade Assistance*, ed. O. Cadot, A. Fernandes, J. Gourdon, and A. Mattoo, 163–182. Washington, DC: World Bank.

Disdier, Anne-Célia, and Stéphan Marette. 2009. "The Combination of Gravity and Welfare Approaches for Evaluating Non-Tariff Measures." INRA working paper 2009-13, French National Institute of Agricultural Research (INRA), Paris.

———. 2010. "How Do Consumers in Developed Countries Value the Environment and Workers' Social Rights in Developing Countries?" *Food Policy* 37 (1): 1–11.

Dixit, Avinash, and R. Pyndick. 1994. *Investment Under Uncertainty*. Princeton, NJ: Princeton University Press.

Ferrantino, Michael. 2006. "Quantifying the Trade and Economic Effects of Non-Tariff Measures." OECD Trade Policy Working Paper 28, Organisation for Economic Co-operation and Development, Paris.

Freeman, A. M. 1993. *The Measurement of Environmental and Resource Values: Theory and Methods*. Washington, DC: Resources for the Future.

Hammitt, James K. 2002. "QALYS versus WTP." *Risk Analysis* 22 (5): 985–1001.

Henry, Claude. 1974. "Investment Decisions Under Uncertainty: The Irreversibility Effect.'" *American Economic Review* 64 (6): 1006–12.

Kee, Hiau Looi, A. Nicita, and M. Olarreaga. 2009. "Estimating Trade Restrictiveness Indices." *Economic Journal* 119 (534): 172–99.

Latacz-Lohman, Uwe, and S. Schilizzi. 2005. "Auctions for Conservation Contracts: A Review of the Theoretical and Empirical Literature." Report to the Scottish Executive Environment and Rural Affairs Department. Edinburgh, U.K.: Government of Scotland.

List, John. 2006. "Field Experiments: A Bridge between Lab and Naturally Occurring Data." *B.E. Journal of Economic Analysis and Policy* 6 (2): 1–45.

Marette, Stéphan, J. Roosen, S. Blanchemanche, and P. Verger. 2008. "The Choice of Fish Species: An Experiment Measuring the Impact of Risk and Benefit Information." *Journal of Agricultural and Resource Economics* 33 (1): 1–18.

McLinden, Gerard, E. Fanta, D. Widdowson, and T. Doyle. 2011. *Border Management Modernization: A Practical Guide for Reformers*. Washington, DC: World Bank.

Noussair, Charles., S. Robin, and B. Ruffieux. 2002. "Do Consumers Not Care about Biotech Foods or Do They Just Not Read the Labels?" *Economics Letters* 75 (1): 47–53.

Otsuki, Tsunehiro, J. Wilson, and M. Sewadeh. 2001. "Saving Two in a Billion: Quantifying the Trade Effect of European Food Safety Standards on African Exports." *Food Policy* 26: 495–514.

Pimentel, David, L. Lach, R. Zuniga, and D. Morrison. 2000. "Environmental and Economic Costs of Nonindigenous Species in the United States." *Bioscience* 50 (1): 53–65.

Pimentel, David, R. Zuniga, and D. Morrison. 2005. "Update on the Environmental and Economic Costs Associated with Alien-Invasive Species in the United States." *Ecological Economics* 52 (3): 273–88.

Rodrik, Dani. 1987. "Policy Targeting with Endogenous Distortions: Theory of Optimum Subsidy." *Quarterly Journal of Economics* 102 (4): 903–11.

Stoneham, Gary, V. Chaudry, A. Ha, and L. Strappazzon. 2003. "Auctions for Conservation Contracts: An Empirical Examination of Victoria's BushTender Trial." *Australian Journal of Agricultural and Resource Economics* 47 (4): 477–500.

van Tongeren, Frank, J. Beghin, and S. Marette. 2009. "A Cost-Benefit Framework for the Assessment of Non-Tariff Measuers in Agro-Food Trade." OECD Food, Agriculture and Fisheries Working Paper 21, Organisation for Economic Co-operation and Development, Paris.

Viscusi, W. Kip. 1993. "The Value of Risks to Life and Death." *Journal of Economic Literature* 31 (4): 1912–46.

CHAPTER 3

Streamlining NTMs: Processes and Institutions

Countries have adopted a number of approaches to streamlining non-tariff measures (NTMs), but no best practice has yet emerged. The method depends on specific conditions such as the legal context, existing institutional arrangements, and the financial and human resources available. This chapter reviews streamlining methods used to date. A comprehensive regulatory reform should start with full regulatory impact assessments (RIAs) for existing and proposed NTMs, subject to reviews during the design and application of the measure by other agencies. However, because implementing a comprehensive regulatory reform is not always politically feasible, this chapter provides different options for design of a review process to gradually initiate reforms that eventually will result in a set of regulatory best practices for streamlining NTMs, including the introduction of regulatory impact assessments.[1]

Whatever legal arrangement a country may choose, one common principle for success is that the review process not be conducted exclusively by the agency responsible for issuing the regulation but involve other agencies as well. This chapter will discuss basic requirements for all involved in the review process.

Getting the Institutional Setup Right

Regulatory reforms require a great deal of political capital, and their political economy is usually complex (IFC 2010; OECD 2009).[2] International experience helps define the basic requirements for the NTM review process (figure 3.1). The political support and commitment of the government and all relevant authorities involved in the process must be secured (see also Akinci and Ladegaard 2009; Jacobs and Ladegaard 2010). Box 3.1 describes Brazil's efforts to introduce best regulatory practice in a program of regulatory impact assessments. Thus the institutional arrangement to conduct the review has better chances to succeed if (1) it is driven by a high level of the administration with the appropriate mandate (supported by law or decree); (2) it involves all stakeholders concerned; (3) it ensures the participation of the highest officials responsible for the issuing and administration of the measures, including the agency's staff; and (4) finally, it has the necessary technical and financial resources to conduct its mandate, which means that the officials involved in the regulatory process must receive the training and skill improvement as well as the tools to perform their tasks.

Strong political support is essential to achieve results and effectiveness—more than any formal basis such as law, decree, directive, or resolutions—to provide the institutional setup to lead the review process (OECD 2009). This is exemplified by the case of the Republic of Korea and Mexico where political commitment was a key driver of regulatory

Figure 3.1   Political Commitment and NTM Reforms

prevalence/severity of NTM

	few NTMs		many NTMs	
	relatively inocuous	severe	relatively inocuous	severe
strong		full review with institutional setup	systematic, light review	guillotine approach
		Mauritius		*Korea, Rep.; Mexico*
weak				ad hoc—start with low-hanging fruit

political commitment (left axis label)

Source: Authors.

Box 3.1

Brazil Challenges in Regulatory Reforms: Some Preliminary Lessons

Brazil is starting to improve its regulatory practices, including the adoption of regulatory impact assessments (RIAs). In Brazil, the Casa Civil is an organism of the Presidency that is in charge of the PRO-REG (*Programa de Fortalecimento da Capacidade Institucional para a Gestão em Regulação*[a]). The PRO-REG is focused in promoting and implementing RIAs in Brazilian regulatory agencies and has been working in cooperation with the International Development Bank (IDB).

Several agencies are taking part of this initiative, such as *Agencia Nacional de Vigilancia Sanitaria* (ANVISA), *Agencia Nacional do Petroleo, Gas Natural e Biocombustiveis* (ANP), *Agencia Nacional de Energia Electrica* (ANEEL), *Agencia Nacional de Cinema* (ANCINE), and *Instituto Nacional de Metrologia, Qualidade, e Tecnologia* (INMETRO). ANVISA deals with public health and counts on a highly skilled staff, which has been able to promote this agency as one of the most proactive in Brazil and to take it to the vanguard in terms of pursuing regulatory quality. So, these particular features certainly help to explain its early advances in developing a model for RIA implementation. INMETRO has also been recognized as a Brazilian agency that has a very significant and wide role in technical regulation, and which counts on a highly skilled staff to achieve that goal. Therefore, INMETRO has early established requirements on technical reports to give support to the establishment of technical regulations and conformity assessment programs. This agency has been applying a tool called Analysis of Technical and Economic Viability, which consists of an RIA approach used particularly in INMETRO's conformity assessment programs.

Although this is an ongoing process, some preliminary lessons are as follows. First, this experience confirms the importance of the staff availability to implement RIA and cost-benefit analysis (CBA) and the specific skills required to quantify economic, social, and environmental impacts. Staff size and deadlines to develop the studies need to be correlated; thus if deadlines are short, more people must be assigned to the task.

Second, the characteristics of regulatory institutions are critical. A requirement for succeeding in establishing RIAs is to take into consideration the administrative structure of the agency conducting the process in terms of hierarchy, how tasks are distributed and shared, and individual competencies. Above all, it is important

(continued next page)

Box 3.1   *(continued)*

to have a clear diagnostic of the institutional infrastructure before implementing the RIA.

A third important factor is financial resources. Improvements in staff, databases, and infrastructure are dependent on the availability of financial resources. The competition for financial resources might compromise the development and implementation of new tools for RIAs, even though these tools could provide gains in optimizing the allocation of public budget.

Another important issue is that this kind of initiative to quantify and qualify the effects of regulations and propose scenarios to policy makers is only possible if cooperation is achieved among the different governmental agencies, research institutes and universities, and, especially, the private sectors represented by their organizations and other representative organisms. A network of experts is a way to pursue a faster advance in this arena.

Source: de Miranda 2012.
a. In English, literally, Program to Strengthen the Institutional Capacity for Regulatory Management. More information can be found at http://www.regulacao.gov.br/.

reform. In other cases, weaker political support explains the relatively modest progress in the NTM review agenda.

All these review mechanisms start and evolve with political support, but could be disrupted when that support weakens. To support a politically independent, long-term process, the private sector and other interested parties should be allowed a more active role. This is consistent with the idea that a broad base constituency for reform is required (Akinci and Ladegaard 2009; Jacobs and Ladegaard 2010). The mechanisms described offer comprehensive top-down approaches which, although they may be useful for undertaking a radical reform process, do not necessarily build a continuous permanent review process. Building an ongoing program to review and streamline NTMs in the long term should be seen as a continuous and gradual process that can also be complemented by other mechanisms (see appendix A). In this regard, ideally, government should strive to introduce changes and formalize new procedures that promote regulatory quality reforms.

Depending on each country's legal environment—the level of the regulations (laws, decrees, administrative decisions, and so on), the level of the authority involved (national, subnational, or municipal), or the entity responsible for issuing the regulation—the NTM review process can be more complex when it involves working with different legal mandates, more decision layers, and more stakeholders. Consequently the existing institutional arrangements for reviewing NTMs may not be appropriate for this level of complexity. The proposal for NTM review outlined in this chapter could be implemented at different government levels, but flexibility should be considered when assessing the final approach in a specific country context.

The second condition for a successful NTM review is the choice of the review body or ministry to conduct it. International experience with regulatory actions to improve domestic competitiveness shows that the reviewing body must be provided with adequate independence and authority to conduct the review apart from the agencies responsible for issuing the regulations (Akinci and Ladegaard 2009; Jacobs and Ladegaard 2010). Effective results are more limited when the review is conducted by an internal unit within the regulatory agency because regulators tend to want to keep their regulations in place. However, if such institutional design is not politically feasible, the reviewing unit should be located in a ministry politically and technically strong enough to conduct the process. For instance, in some countries, such as Australia and New Zealand, the review process for new regulations is conducted within the Finance Ministry. More recently, the government of Mauritius has established a joint public-private business facilitation task force to coordinate and strengthen the review process for business regulations and procedures, including a committee dedicated to the review of NTMs. The reviewing body is also ultimately responsible for the work and reporting requirements of the review. Another option is to create an interagency committee to conduct the review, as in Japan, which has a Regulatory Reform Ministerial Council, and in Mexico, where a specialized public agency oversees the regulatory formation process.

Third, the review body selected must be given sufficient resources to thoroughly review the regulations (Jacobs and Ladegaard 2010). Experience shows that lack of resources can jeopardize the process when the entity is not capable of conducting complex reviews itself due to lack of staffing and skills and does not have sufficient resources to outsource such reviews.

Fourth, beyond existing measures, the responsibility for improving the overall regulatory environment goes beyond a single unit and is a continuous process. This means that the NTM review process must involve all regulatory agencies and they must have best regulatory practices incorporated in their working procedures (IFC 2010).

Regulatory agencies address a large range of issues such as sanitary and phytosanitary regulations, the protection of human health, the environment, and safety. Depending on countries' regulatory structure, these topics may fall within the responsibility of different ministries or independent entities. The review body responsible for the review must also have the following responsibilities:

- Define the general principles of regulatory reform based on international best practice and ensure that these are applied consistently across line ministries and departments.
- Oversee the introduction of regulatory impact analysis as a key tool across the government.
- Facilitate the inter-ministerial coordination that is essential to address a wide range of complex multidisciplinary regulatory issues.
- Ensure transparency and public dissemination of existing regulations, including their policy objectives and rationale, and provide technical background information that supports the rationale for the regulations.

Figure 3.2 illustrates one possible institutional setup—in this case a review committee integrated by ministries and relevant agencies responsible for regulatory matters—for reviewing NTMs as part of a broader agenda of regulatory review of business regulations.

When the proposed institutional setup is not feasible because of political factors or is not possible in the short term, the review process could be developed exclusively within the existing institutional framework. This would require locating the review process within the agencies responsible for issuing the regulations. For example, Australian authorities mandate a review process within each regulatory agency, such as the Department of Agriculture, Fisheries, and Forestry; Department of Health and Ageing; the Treasury; and the Reserve Bank of Australia, among others. In order to achieve the broader goal of regulatory reform, the resources should focus on strengthening the regulatory agencies. More specifically this will require introducing the NTM review process as part of the regulatory process, establishing a transparent and participatory process that will ensure accountability, and improving staff skills and knowledge on regulatory matters within the regulatory agency. The Indonesian government has just adopted a decree to institutionalize the review process for the introduction of new NTMs (see box 3.2). While

Figure 3.2   Sample Institutional Setup for NTM Review

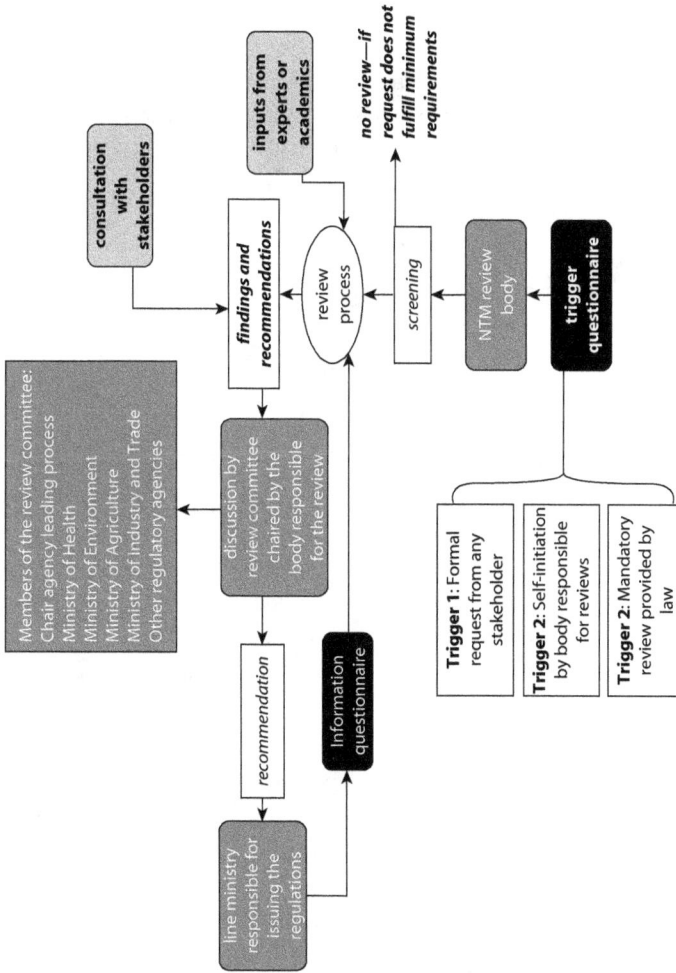

Members of the review committee:
Chair agency leading process
Ministry of Health
Ministry of Environment
Ministry of Agriculture
Ministry of Industry and Trade
Other regulatory agencies

consultation with stakeholders

inputs from experts or academics

no review—if request does not fulfill minimum requirements

findings and recommendations

review process

screening

NTM review body

trigger questionnaire

discussion by review committee chaired by the body responsible for the review

recommendation

Information questionnaire

line ministry responsible for issuing the regulations

Trigger 1: Formal request from any stakeholder

Trigger 2: Self-initiation by body responsible for reviews

Trigger 2: Mandatory review provided by law

Source: Authors.

Box 3.2

Institutional Setup to Streamline New NTMs in Indonesia

Streamlining NTMs in Indonesia received a new impetus from the Ministry of Trade in September 2011, which launched a pilot program establishing a review process for NTMs issued by this ministry, currently responsible for 61 percent of all NTMs issued (see chapter 4 for an in-depth discussion of Indonesia's experience with streamlining NTMs). The main thrust of the program is to remove the NTM review process from the unit that implements NTMs and to equip a new unit with adequate capacity to conduct RIAs. The decree establishes a Non-Tariff Policy (NTP) Team within the Ministry of Trade whose tasks are to (1) coordinate with relevant agencies for input into the formulation and establishment of NTMs; (2) formulate and submit recommendations to the Minister of Trade on NTM policies; (3) monitor and evaluate the implementation of NTM policies; (4) introduce NTM policies to stakeholders; and (5) participate in international trade negotiations in the framework of bilateral, regional, and multilateral cooperation with implications for Indonesia's NTM policies.

The ministry also introduced a standard operating procedure (SOP) for reviewing NTMs (see figure 3.3) to conduct objective and independent assessments within a specified time. The team will analyze the eligibility of a proposed NTM; analyze potential impacts of a proposed NTM using appropriate analytical tools; verify the proposed NTM's consistency with other national policies and with the WTO rules or other international agreements; and hold a public consultation through meetings with stakeholders or field surveys. The NTP Team should reach a conclusion regarding the NTM within a maximum of 60 working days.

this toolkit focuses on the review of existing NTMs, such institutional setups may be appropriate for reviewing both existing and new NTMs.

Finally, the single most important way for countries to improve their regulatory environment is to enhance transparency. Strict transparency requirements provide important information regarding the nature of existing regulations, their objectives, and whether they are based on international standards and recommendations (for instance, from the International Organization for Standardization [ISO]), among other aspects. Transparency is usually an international requirement embedded in agreements such as the WTO, as well as regional and bilateral trade agreements the countries must comply with. Usually, the establishment of an enquiry point, for example, located at the Trade Ministry or the

Figure 3.3 SOPs for Introducing NTMs in the Indonesia Ministry of Trade

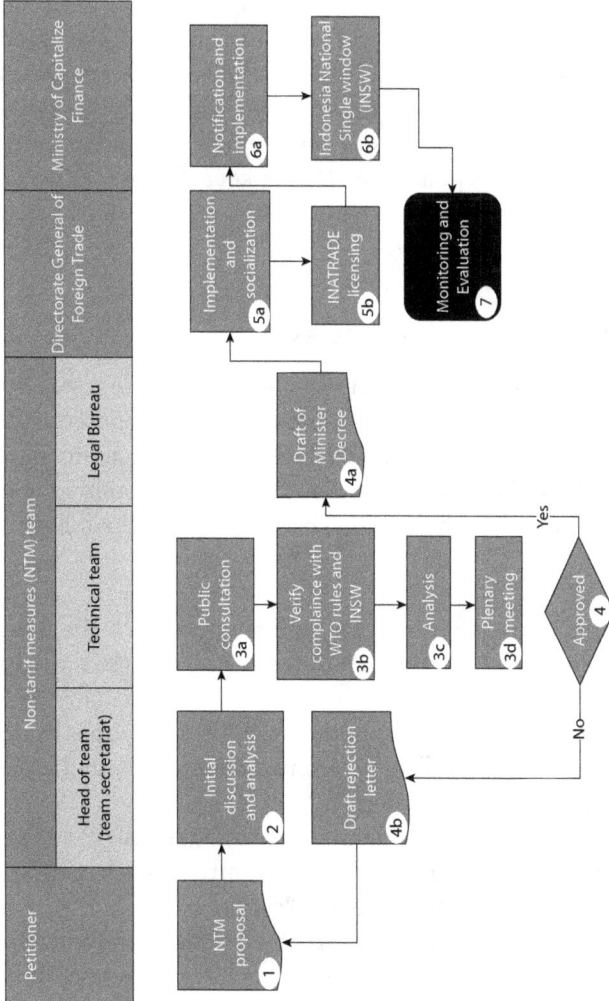

Source: Authors.
Notes: Numbers indicate the flow of steps. DGFT = Directorate General of Foreign Trade; INSW = Indonesia Single Window.

Agriculture Ministry, to answer questions about regulations, including proposed regulations, is mandatory, but countries may wish to adopt additional transparency rules beyond those required by international agreements. For instance, they could ensure that proposed new regulations or changes to existing regulations are publicized and ample opportunity for comments and suggestions for domestic and international interested parties are provided. Enhancement of transparency has been facilitated in recent years by information and communication technologies that have lowered the costs of improved access to relevant information as well as the costs to provide and manage information. Moreover, transparency is both an important driver as well as a supporter of regulatory reform; increased transparency reduces policy risks for market actors as well as the potential capture of regulators by interested parties (Akinci and Ladegaard 2009; Jacobs and Ladegaard 2010).

Steps in the NTM Review Process

To establish a review process for existing NTMs the first step is to identify the organization, mandate, and working procedures necessary to conduct the review. The approach should be flexible to accommodate different review methodologies that take into account the country's specific environment. The approach described here is based on the following working principles:

1. The primary responsibility for regulation lies with the issuing regulatory agency/ministry. The aim of the review process is to support their work.
2. The review process aims at improving trade regulations by determining whether they are fulfilling their stated objectives with the least possible restriction of trade.
3. The review process should be led by a body, ministry, or committee (or interministerial or interagency committee) with a clear mandate, accountability, and strong political support.
4. The review favors a gradual approach to regulatory reform that is sustainable over time and aims at establishing a review process that can grow over time (see also IFC 2010). Gradualism means that the review process could initially focus on specific institutions (for example, standard-setting bodies) or regulations (for example, prohibitions, licensing or other prima facie trade barriers) and later on move to wider issues. The final goal is that countries adopt wide regulatory reforms to implement

ex-ante best regulatory practices, including regulatory impact assessments.

5. The initiation of the review process should be substantiated to avoid using resources on irrelevant requests. In order to achieve this, the proposal provides for minimum requirements to initiate and conduct the review (aiming to avoid frivolous requests).

6. The review process should proceed as an ex-post RIA insofar as it must provide an analysis of the costs and benefits of the measure in place to allow for an informed decision by the authorities responsible for the review as well as the agency/ministry responsible for issuing the regulations as to whether a measure should be maintained, changed, or eliminated according to the review findings.

7. A final objective of the review is to assess, as far as possible, the actual result of the regulations, that is, the degree of consistency between ex-ante assessments of regulatory impacts and the actual, or ex-post, impacts (OECD 2009).

Planning a Dedicated NTM Review Process

The NTM review process should begin with an independent regulatory review by an entity separate from the one responsible for issuing regulations.[3] It could be an existing ministry, as in New Zealand where the Treasury department is responsible for reviewing new regulations, or a specialized body such as COFEMER in Mexico that has the specific mandate to conduct RIAs (box 3.3).

The NTM review process should involve wide consultation to hear and reflect the views of all concerned parties, principally the regulatory agencies responsible for regulations, representatives from the private sector affected by the measure, and representatives of civil society. Consultation helps mitigate the complexity of changes in the political economy context. Participation provides access to information that may not be readily available to authorities responsible for issuing and administering regulations and reduces the pressure exerted on the authorities.

The NTM review process is information-intensive. The unit responsible for the review must gather a wide range of information from various sources (private, public, confidential, non-confidential, scientific and non-scientific, hard data and anecdotal evidence). Usually, the information will be difficult to gather and process, not least to weigh. Therefore, the overall review process must be transparent and facilitate access to and assessment of the information that supports the review of the measure. In order to achieve this, the body responsible must be accountable for its work.

Box 3.3

Regulatory Reform in Mexico

Mexico's COFEMER (*Comisión Federal de Mejora Regulatoria*) RIA program was consolidated and detailed in reforms to the Administrative Procedures Act in 2000, which were greatly influenced by the Economic Deregulation Unit's five years of experience in the review of regulations and international best practices. The main aspects of the program were:

- The presidential appointment of the COFEMER head and the granting of technical autonomy to the institution.
- The creation of the Federal Council for Regulatory Improvement as a means of ensuring the accountability of COFEMER and giving the business, labor, and academic sectors an important role in the direction of the reform program's work program.
- Requiring each ministry and regulatory agency to name a vice-minister in charge of coordinating in-house regulatory reform efforts, and of submitting two-year work programs to COFEMER for review and public comment.
- Implementing a detailed RIA review process and a mandatory minimum 30-day period of public comment for all regulations. COFEMER can question and require more detailed analysis of RIAs within 10 working days of submission and has 30 working days to issue its opinion on the proposal itself. Ministries and agencies must publicly respond to all COFEMER comments and suggestions.

To enhance transparency and provide guidance on how to conduct RIAs, COFEMER developed an electronic platform that allowed for the centralization of communication between COFEMER and the vice-ministry in charge of regulatory reform in each institution, easy access to technical reference materials, and prompt publication of relevant consultation documents. The online RIA template includes sections on the following:

- The description of the regulatory action, identifying the nature of the problem and risks that each proposal seeks to address.
- Legal analysis, including a clear review of powers, and compatibility with the existing regulatory framework.
- Alternatives considered (both regulatory and non-regulatory), and an explanation of how the proposal is considered to be the least intrusive option to attain the stated goals.

(continued next page)

Box 3.3 *(continued)*

- Implementation strategy and the consideration of resources necessary to ensure proper compliance and supervision.
- Quantifiable and non-quantifiable costs and benefits of the proposal. In addition to requiring explicit consideration of effects on market competition, domestic and international trade, small and medium size enterprises, and consumer access to goods and services, the RIA process requires that all relevant capital, operation, and transaction costs, and the effects on health, safety, and the environment be itemized.

Source: Haddou 2012.

The findings of the review should be informed to a higher authority that will take the final politically informed decisions. Figure 3.4 summarizes the requirements for conducting the review.

The mandate of the reviewer. Once it is determined which body will be responsible for conducting the NTM review, the government will define the scope of the mandate, the substantial nature of the review, and its objectives. Although this body will lead the process, all relevant regulatory bodies should be involved in the review process and the review of the facts as well as the analysis of the work conducted by the review body,

The mandate of the body responsible for leading the review is as follows:

1. Propose the procedures for conducting a review.
2. Undertake the review in a reasonable period of time. Depending on the measures, for example, licenses or prohibitions, the reviews may be shorter. In other cases, for example, for measures dealing with health or environmental protection, the review may require a longer time.
3. Verify the accuracy and adequacy of the request review.
4. Inform the pertinent authority of the reviews undertaken, ongoing, and expected.
5. Gather information, including sending questionnaire to stakeholder to request specific information.
6. Organize hearings with stakeholders to discuss the information gathered.

Figure 3.4 Review Process Flow

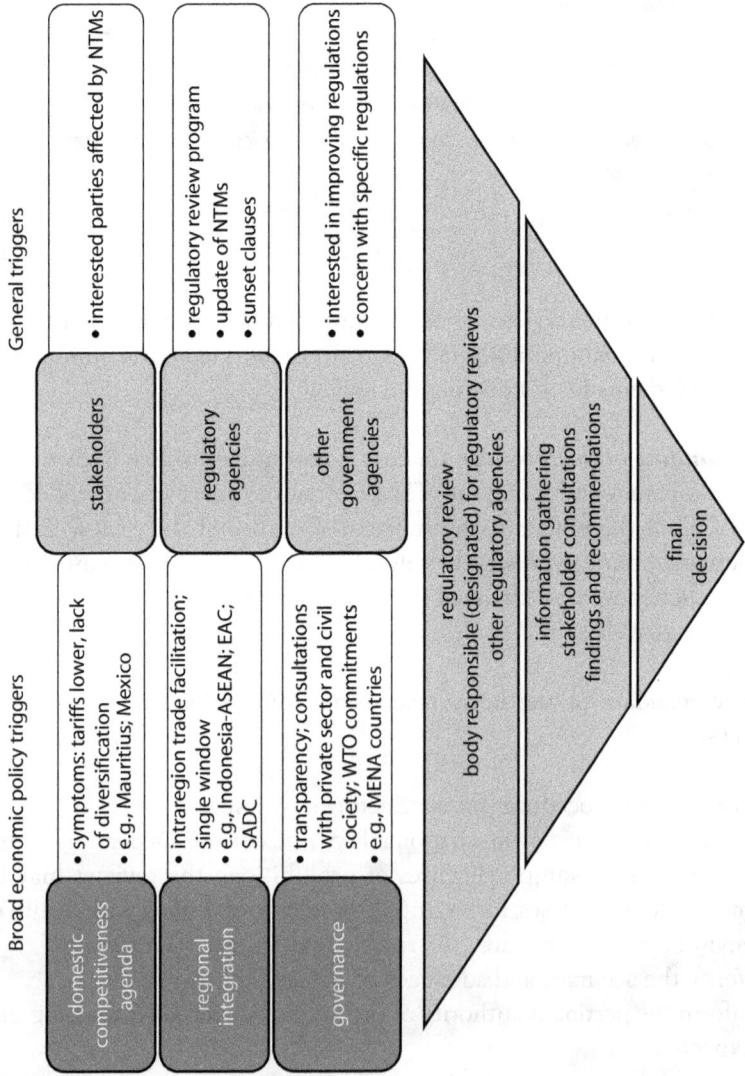

Broad economic policy triggers

General triggers

domestic competitiveness agenda	• symptoms: tariffs lower, lack of diversification • e.g., Mauritius; Mexico
regional integration	• intraregion trade facilitation; single window • e.g., Indonesia-ASEAN; EAC; SADC
governance	• transparency: consultations with private sector and civil society; WTO commitments • e.g., MENA countries

stakeholders	• interested parties affected by NTMs
regulatory agencies	• regulatory review program • update of NTMs • sunset clauses
other government agencies	• interested in improving regulations • concern with specific regulations

regulatory review
body responsible (designated) for regulatory reviews
other regulatory agencies

information gathering
stakeholder consultations
findings and recommendations

final decision

Source: Authors.
Notes: ASEAN = Association of Southeast Asian Nations; EAC = East African Community; SADC = Southern African Development Community; MENA = Middle Eastern and North African.

7. Coordinate the review process with all regulatory agencies.
8. Issue a report, in principle within a 60–90 day period after receiving a review request.
9. Present an annual report summarizing the activities undertaken and proposing a work program for the following year.

Key considerations in planning the NTM review process are (see Australia Government 2010; New Zealand Government 2009):

- The rationale (or objectives) of the existing regulation being reviewed; specifically, the review should focus on the reasons to regulate, that is, the market failure the regulation aims to address.
- Whether those objectives and problems were adequately met by the regulation, including any expected impacts.
- An analysis of possible alternative means to reach the objectives in a less trade restrictive manner and its possible costs, including enforcement costs of the options considered as well as likely impact on competition in the market.
- Findings and recommendations.

Note that the review does not change which agency is ultimately responsible for enforcing the regulation in a specific area (health, environment technical barriers to trade, or SPS measures, and so on). The reviewing body must maintain a delicate balance between reviewing other agencies' regulations and performing its own regulatory responsibilities. While the reviewing body's findings should include both an assessment and a recommendation at a technical level, the final decision on whether to maintain, alter, or eliminate the measure is a political decision and under the purview of the issuing regulatory authority.

Conducting the Review Process
Given the political economy and the information-intensive nature of the NTM review process, defining clear triggers for initiating reviews is important (see figure 3.4). It is crucial that the process focus on important regulations in terms of competitiveness benefits and avoid wasting scarce resources. As such, this toolkit offers a few triggers for launching or initiating ex-post reviews (see IFC 2010).

Comprehensive and systematic reviews. A comprehensive review process is often launched by a political decision to undertake reforms with the aims of reducing the quantity of regulations, eliminating duplications, reducing the time and costs of excessive regulations, and improving the regulatory environment (Akinci and Ladegaard 2009; Jacobs and Ladegaard 2010). The methods used in this approach are re-engineering processes, the Standard Cost Model, the guillotine, the bulldozer, scrap-and-build, and staged repeal or "automatic revocation," described in the annex to this chapter. The methods have been used with varying degrees of success in different contexts, and they can be an effective mechanism to radically transform inefficient or outmoded regulatory environments (IFC 2010). These methods are usually related to a broader reform process, such as improving competitiveness and governance, accession to multilateral organization, or as part of a regional integration agenda such as that being carried out by the Association of Southeast Asian Nations (see figure 3.4).

For instance, in Mexico, although COFEMER is the body responsible for ex-ante review of regulations issued by the competent authorities, recently the government undertook a review process led by the Ministry of Economy and the Ministry of Public Administration. The "Zero Base Regulation Approach" conducts a comprehensive review of all business regulations and identifies those that need to be reformed or eliminated. The regulatory simplification process involves eight ministries and should be fully implemented by early 2012. The Mexican Government expects these changes to save about 0.4 percent of GDP per year (World Bank 2010).

In other countries, the regulatory review of specific regulations is embedded in the domestic legal system and follows a more gradual approach for reviews (IFC 2010; OECD 2009). For example, a clause may require that reviews be conducted within a certain period of time after the entry into force of a regulation. The basic principle is that a measure will continue to be applied unless action is taken to eliminate it. The action means to integrate a clause in the regulation that will lead to its review and possible legal cancellation. Another mechanism is sunset clauses in which new regulations are given automatic expiration dates, unless rewritten through normal rulemaking processes. Sunset clauses ensure that review of a regulation takes place after a specific period of time. For example, in Australia, since 2006 most subordinate regulations (where the parliament has delegated regulation-making powers to a minister, person, or organizations) automatically sunset after 10 years (Australian Government 2010).

The founding principle in the ex-post review process proposed here is that those affected (or interested) by the regulations are in a better position to take the initiative for the reviews without waiting for a government action. One weakness of this approach, though, is that it relies on the initiative of interested, usually private sector, parties. The question is how to ensure that badly needed reviews will take place even when society may have conflicting interests with regard to existing regulations.

In order to ensure that reviews will be undertaken, the body responsible for reviews should (1) identify and propose reviews of measures that potentially affect businesses or investments and (2) reach out to the private sector, academics, and other interested parties to identify priority regulations to be reviewed.

In addition, governments may mandate that each agency responsible for issuing regulations must propose an annual review plan, and all regulations that are not subject to sunset clauses or review clauses must be reviewed every five years. When an agency does not contemplate any review, it must justify the decision (Australian Government 2010).

Reviews requested by interested parties. A review of an NTM may be initiated upon a request from an interested party. In such a case, some guiding principles should be met. A review to determine the impact of NTMs on trade can be initiated upon a written request by or on behalf of the domestic industry, or any interested party, or any government agency, or by the body responsible for the review on its own initiative.[4] A request shall include the following:

- The governmental measure/regulation affects trade;
- It has been in place at least three years;
- Evidence on how the measure impacts trade;
- Preliminary analysis of the measure's costs, benefits, and risks; and
- Evidence of the causality between the measure and the trade impact.

The application shall contain such information as is reasonably available to the applicant on the following:

- Identity of the applicant (including all names and contact information);
- A description of the volume and value of the domestic production affected by the measure (where a written application is made on behalf of the domestic industry, the application shall identify the industry on behalf of which the application is made, or associations of domestic producers);

- A general description of the measure and products affected, including import and exports; and
- Information regarding the nature of the adverse effects that arise from the measure or the compliance mechanisms in place (in addition to the interventions already in place), and identify other potential affected parties.

The reviewing body would then conduct a preliminary check to verify the accuracy and adequacy of the information provided in the application to determine whether the evidence is sufficient to justify the initiation of a review. An application could be rejected and a review could be terminated promptly as soon as the body decides so, on the basis of a written notice to the interested party, and if it is satisfied that there is not sufficient evidence for proceeding with the review.[5] The criteria for assessing whether to initiate a review or not include whether the measure clearly restricts trade (for example, prohibitions and quantity restrictions); whether the impact is large; whether the industry affected by the existing regulation contributes largely to the economy (GDP, employment, foreign reserves); and whether the measure affects a minority or a special group of citizens. A standard questionnaire for such an application can be found in appendix B.

Output of the Review Process

The body responsible for the review collects the information, conducts an analysis of the cost and benefit of regulations, and makes a recommendation on whether to keep the regulation as is, change the legal text and/or the enforcement of the regulation, or remove/replace the regulation.

A final report will reflect the findings of the following tasks and the findings of the review:[6]

1. Define the problem.
2. State the public policy objectives of the reviewed measure.
3. Identify and analyze the reviewed measure, including whether it is clear and concisely written.
4. Analyze the trade-related impact of the measure through a cost-benefit analysis or equivalent technique.
5. Analyze the incidence: who bears the costs and benefits—for example, small business compared to medium and large, exporters versus importing substitution firms—of the trade-related impacts of the measure.

6. Make an assessment of other available policy options, their incidence, and how they could achieve a less trade-restrictive outcome while maintaining the same level of protection; due consideration of the difference on impact incidence depending on the options should be considered as well.

7. Include the following implementation issues:
   - Administration issues, such as which agency is responsible for the administration of the options and resources available.
   - The information that regulated parties will require in order to comply with the regulation.
   - Timing and transitional arrangements, for example, gradual introduction of new requirements, at least six months before the entry into force of the new regulation, provision of interim assistance.
   - Enforcement strategy to include how compliance can be enforced and the suitability of risk-based enforcement strategies.

8. Describe the consultation process undertaken during the review.

9. Present the overall assessment, including the findings and the policy recommendation to maintain, change, or remove a measure.

Before a final determination is made, the body will inform all interested parties of the essential facts under consideration which form the basis for the recommendation regarding the reviewed measure.

The final report may recommend maintaining, changing, or eliminating the measure. If the recommendation is to change or eliminate the measure, it should be referred to the competent authority.

Annex: Approaches to Streamlining Existing NTMs

Countries have pursued different strategies to review NTMs with variable success. Two broad tool categories have been identified: fast track and non-fast track tools. The first category focuses on tackling "quick wins," that is, reforms that further support a broader review process to simplify regulations and reduce their burden. The second category, non-fast track tools, focuses on the more systemic problems related to regulations, including changing the administrative culture (IFC 2010).[7]

Fast-Track Tools

The **Standard Cost Model** (SCM) measures the administrative burdens imposed on businesses through legislation, regulations, and other requirements. The SCM helps to identify which regulations are causing the greatest burden and to establish a priority agenda of reform. The model can be used to measure the cost of information obligations arising from different sources, such as all existing laws and regulations; specific laws and regulations such as fiscal rules, transport sector regulations, starting a business, or employment procedures; or specific requirements imposed by a selected government body. To determine the costs to businesses, administrative compliance costs are calculated, including number of businesses subject to the requirement, frequency of filings, and costs of engaging employees and external service providers in these activities. Once the costs are determined, a reduction target can be defined for authorities in order to reduce those costs. Using this method in developing countries may be difficult because the amount of data that may be required is usually not available. However, according to IFC (2010), this limitation may be overcome by reducing the data requirements without significant accuracy losses.

In the **guillotine method,** the review process consists of counting and then reviewing a large number of regulations against specified criteria. This tool is based on the principle of the "reversal of burden of proof," whereby the regulators must justify why a regulation is needed or else remove it. This approach is systematic and transparent and does not require lengthy and costly legal action on each regulation. The guillotine approach is a fast and less costly review process when a large number of regulations are involved. It has been usually recommended when countries are undertaking significant reforms in moving toward more open market economies.

The bulldozer approach is a bottom-up process that involves empowering business communities to identify unnecessary regulations and advocate for reform or removal at different levels of government, including lower levels such as municipal and regional agencies. It is called "bulldozer" because it empowers local communities to confront and remove obstacles previously considered impregnable to public concern. This process has two goals: to bulldoze a dense forest of regulations and to create a permanent dialogue and partnership between the private sector and the government. One of its shortcomings, though, is that it does not necessarily provide for a change in the regulatory process.

Non-Fast-Track Tools
Process re-engineering consists of a review of the business procedures required by government aiming at improving their efficiency, effectiveness,

and transparency. Process re-engineering can be accomplished through three components: (1) identification and redesign of procedures, (2) elimination of unnecessary steps, and (3) application of information technology. Usually, licenses and permit reforms are the most popular targets of process reengineering as they impose heavy burdens on investment, business start-up, existing businesses, and public administration workload.

Scrap-and-build is a complete review of the regulatory system, rethinking its principles and the interactions between regulators. In 1995, the Dutch government established a Functioning of Markets, Deregulation and Legislative Quality Program that used this approach, deregulating a wide range of activities, such as liberalization of professions and harmonizing food legislation (IFC 2010).

Staged repeal or "automatic revocation" is a progressive, staggered schedule of review and repeal of regulations based on their date of adoption. Regulations are given a systematic and comprehensive review after a designated time period and either renewed, remade, or repealed by expiry. The aim is to eliminate unnecessary or out-of-date regulations and at the same time to modernize the regulations that addresses existing problems. This tool has been applied by a limited number of countries, usually of a common law tradition such as Australia, Canada, and New Zealand. However, this procedure may be costly and complex to implement in developing countries.

Review and sunset clauses: Review clauses are requirements in regulations for review to be conducted within a certain period. The basic principle of this tool is the following: a rule will continue to be applied unless action is taken to eliminate it. The action means to integrate a clause in the regulation that will lead to its review and possible legal cancellation. By contrast, "sunsetting" is a process in which new regulations are given automatic expiration dates, unless remade through normal rulemaking processes. This ensures continuing review and updating of the stock of regulations.

Notes

1. Best regulatory practices are explained in chapter 1.
2. Other factors to be considered when engaged in wide regulatory reform, such as the importance of external pressure and taking advantage of the context in which reforms take place (for instance, in economic crises), are examined in Akinci and Ladegaard (2009).

3. This section describes practices recommended by the Australia Government (2010) and New Zealand Government (2009). Review processes can also be found in many OECD countries.

4. This is a similar process than the one proposed by the WTO agreements that deals with trade remedies investigations. Measures that have no or only minor impacts on businesses or consumers will not be part of the review process.

5. The body could adopt a set of parameters to quickly assess the impact of the barriers such as a de minimis threshold to assess the costs of the measure, to determine whether it is negligible.

6. These topics are similar to those addressed in RIAs (see, for example, Australia Government 2010; New Zealand Government 2009).

7. See IFC (2010) for a complete list with detailed analysis and additional tools not discussed here.

References

Akinci, Gokhan, and Peter Ladegaard. 2009. "Lessons for Reformers: How to Launch, Implement, and Sustain Regulatory Reforms." Working Paper 58694, World Bank, Washington, DC.

Australian Government. 2010. *Best Practice Regulation Handbook*, 2007 and 2010 eds. Canberra: Government of Australia.

de Miranda, Silvia. 2012. "Regulatory Impact Assessment: The Brazilian Experience." In *Non-Tariff Measures—A Fresh Look at Trade Policy's New Frontier*, ed. Olivier Cadot and Mariem Malouche. London/Washington, DC: Centre for Economic Policy Research/World Bank.

Haddou, A. 2012. "Streamlining NTMs: How Mexico Did It." In *Non-Tariff Measures—A Fresh Look at Trade Policy's New Frontier*, ed. Olivier Cadot and Mariem Malouche. London/Washington, DC: Centre for Economic Policy Research/World Bank.

IFC (International Finance Corporation). 2010. "Better Regulation for Growth: Governance Frameworks and Tools for Effective Regulatory Reform—Tools and Approaches to Review Existing Regulations." International Finance Corporation/World Bank, Washington, DC.

Jacobs, S., and P. Ladegaard. 2010. "Regulatory Governance in Developing Countries." International Finance Corporation/World Bank, Washington, DC.

New Zealand Government. 2009. *Regulatory Impact Analysis Handbook*. Wellington: Government of New Zealand, Treasury.

OECD (Organisation for Economic Co-operation and Development). 2009. *Regulatory Impact Analysis: A Tool for Policy Coherence*. Paris: OECD.

Radealli, C. M., and F. De Francesco. 2010. "Regulatory Impact Assessment." In *The Oxford Handbook of Regulation*, ed. Martin Lodge, Martin Cave, and Robert Baldwin, 279–301. Oxford, UK: Oxford University Press.

World Bank. 2010. "Strengthening the Business Environment for Enhanced Economic Growth." Development Policy Loan Report 58431-MX, World Bank, Washington, DC.

CHAPTER 4

Country and Region Experiences with Streamlining NTMs

This chapter describes how some developing countries have managed their non-tariff measure (NTM) reform process, as well as the achievements of regional groups that have actively aimed at the streamlining of NTMs as part of the regional trade facilitation agenda. The challenges faced by policy makers and the solutions achieved will be highlighted in both cases.

Unilaterally Driven Reforms

Mexico, Mauritius, and Indonesia have embarked on the policy agenda of streamlining NTMs, and have done so either unilaterally to strengthen the competitiveness of domestic firms or regionally to abide by regional commitments in preferential trade agreements and to facilitate internal trade. In both cases, policy makers whose programs have achieved results on the ground affirm that the reforms were essential to support domestic business competitiveness. They also typically championed this reform agenda as part of the country's development strategy, giving legal mandates to specific government bodies to lead the reform agenda, thereby sending a strong signal about their firm commitment to supporting the development of a dynamic private sector, in particular small and medium enterprises (SMEs). These policy makers aimed to strengthen the domestic regulatory process and to put in place regulations that would achieve the objectives without creating unnecessary barriers to trade. Streamlining NTMs was also intended to reduce the opacity of regulations by making the information available to the public and private operators and by taking into account the views of all interested parties. As such, the reforms were aimed at improving trade regulations, particularly those that helped with access to information for capacity-constrained SMEs and minorities, in particular in developing countries.

Mexico

Mexico presents an interesting example of a comprehensive, unilaterally driven competitiveness agenda. The Mexican experience also highlights the benefits of streamlining NTMs as part of a broader regulatory reform agenda. Regulatory reform has been a fundamental element of Mexico's transition from a closed to an open market-based economy. The process started in the mid-1980s, when general frustration with macroeconomic instability and years of stagnant growth and inflation in the wake of the 1982 debt crisis led to a revamping of economic policy based on three interdependent pillars: trade liberalization, privatization, and regulatory reform. The change entailed a complete recasting of Mexico's system of regulatory governance, which underwent three main phases, each building on the achievements of the one before.

Phase 1: Planting the seeds for competitiveness and regulatory reform. The progressive trade liberalization began with a significant unilateral reduction of tariffs and import licenses in the framework of Mexico's accession to the General Agreement on Tariffs and Trade in the mid-1980s. The level of protection within the Mexican economy was significantly reduced by 1987: The average tariff reached a historical minimum of 10 percent, down from 27 percent in 1982, and only 27.5 percent of imports remained subject to permit requirements against 100 percent in 1982. Mexico pursued its openness policy through the negotiation of free trade agreements (FTAs) with a large number of partners, including Chile (1992), the Asia Pacific Economic Cooperation (1993), the United States and Canada (1994), Central American economies (1998–99), the European Union (2000), and Japan (2005). By 2005, more than 80 percent of Mexican trade was taking place with preferential partners, and only about 4 percent of imports were subject to permits and licenses (IQOM 2010).

The trade liberalization process went hand in hand with the establishment of new regulatory institutions, tools, and processes intended to make the most of opportunities created by the FTAs and the promotion of the structural reforms—in recently privatized network industries and other areas—needed to boost the productivity and competitiveness of the economy as a whole. Amid preparations for the negotiation of a trade agreement with the United States and Canada, an Economic Deregulation Unit (UDE) was created within the Mexican trade ministry in 1989 to review the national economic regulatory framework. The UDE adopted a reform strategy that aimed to make Mexico's regulatory framework compatible with a modern free-market economy, as well as to reduce operating costs across the board to promote competitiveness.

The reforms were quickly implemented. Between 1989 and 1992, for example, airlines and telephony were privatized; road haulage was deregulated; and private investment—both foreign and domestic—was allowed in road construction, port operation, and electricity generation. The UDE also reviewed over 500 regulatory proposals between 1995 and 2000. The number of licenses, permits, and other information requirements in the commerce and transport sectors, for instance, was cut from about 1,000 in 1995 to fewer than 400 in 2000. All in all, about 90 percent of Mexico's regulatory framework was affected by the process. The UDE used the sense of urgency generated by the economic crisis to its advantage, pushing difficult reforms that might otherwise have failed to generate enough political support. It also greatly helped that the United States government quickly put together a package of over 50 billion dollars in loan guarantees, which would not have been possible without the passage of the North American Free Trade Agreement (NAFTA) (Haddou 2012).[1]

With its long history of poorly designed and inconsistently applied regulations, Mexico also needed to show that its investment environment would be stable and predictable and that NTMs would not be used as a way to get around the treaty's obligations in sensitive sectors.

The UDE stepped in dynamically in 1991–92, designing and promoting four modern laws that have been instrumental in the process of guaranteeing effective market access, transparency, and legal certainty:

- Foreign Trade Law (LCE, *Ley de Comercio Exterior*) specifying, among other things, general tariff, NTM, licensing, quota, safeguards, and antidumping regulations.

- Standards and metrology law, which regulates the establishment of technical rules and standards. It also helped create a more open process for the development of new mandatory technical regulations (NOMs, *Normas Oficial Mexicanas*). The law required the publication of proposed technical rules, and the presentation of cost-benefit analyses to consultative committees comprising public- and private-sector representatives for review and approval. This was the first time that notice-and-comment, as well as cost-benefit analysis, was formally introduced into the Mexican legal system. It completely eliminated the possibility of changing technical rules from one day to the next without giving affected parties an opportunity to comment on the nature and effects of the rules. The process has been improved over the years, but the NOM process was the seed of the regulatory impact assessment (RIA) process.
- Economic competition law, which introduced modern antitrust legislation for the first time in Mexico.
- Industrial property law.

While UDE was set up as a specialized task force to dismantle *existing* regulatory bottlenecks to make the most of a more open trade regime, the LCE established a Commission on Foreign Trade (COCEX, *Comisión de Comercio Exterior*) to review the regulations and to prepare opinions on changes to tariffs, safeguards, antidumping duties, rules of origin requirements, and technical standards relevant to foreign trade. COCEX, which still exists today, is a commission without a permanent structure, comprising representatives from ministries that most often generate NTMs, as well as the foreign affairs ministry, the Bank of Mexico, and the Federal Competition Commission. COCEX was given the power only to issue non-binding opinions (that weren't made public at the time), but it was significant in that it was the first intragovernmental process in the country designed specifically to promote uniformity in domestic trade-related measures and lessen the probability of regulatory capture. Thus, the tandem of UDE and COCEX would tackle existing regulatory bottlenecks and new NTM proposals to avoid entry barriers and unnecessary restrictions on trade.

Nevertheless, there was a strong public backlash as a result of the 1994–95 crisis, fueled by criticisms of lack of transparency and crony capitalism in the privatization of state enterprises and other aspects of economic policy. Support for structural reform began to wane significantly in 1997, the year in which the Institutional Revolutionary Party

(PRI) lost its majority in Congress for the first time in the 20th century. The UDE became keenly aware of the fragility of the regulatory reform process that it had pushed for over a decade. There were a few instances of flagrant non-compliance with the regulatory review process when political pressures overwhelmed the UDE's opposition, and there was mounting and recurrent pressure to tone down or not publicize its opinions, or to expedite the review process.

Phase 2: Regulatory reform agenda at the core of the competitiveness agenda. The euphoria generated by NAFTA was short-lived, as Mexico suffered arguably the worst economic crisis of its modern history in 1995. However, dwindling preferential access to the U.S. market following the rise of China and other nations as direct competitors of Mexico in world markets pointed to the need for moving to higher value-added products and exploiting the geographical proximity to the United States as effective policy options. It became obvious that trade policy alone would not be enough to foster private sector competitiveness and to promote entrepreneurship and a greater industry flexibility. The private sector clamored for government action that would allow for a rapid recovery and a level playing field for companies facing increased competition in the domestic market.

The government responded to the protectionist pressure exercised by the private sector by making business regulatory reform a cornerstone of its "industrial policy." It was identified as an effective—and fiscally inexpensive—business facilitation measure that would complement the devaluation of the peso in helping Mexican companies become internationally competitive. While Mexico remained committed to its preferential commitments, the government did however increase tariffs on imports from the rest of the world over time (up to 15 percent by 2005) to cope with the 1994–95 crisis and appease the private-sector pressure in hardly hit sectors, such as textile and clothing. Mexican President Ernesto Zedillo signed the Agreement for the Deregulation of Economic Activity in 1995 to implement the new regulatory reform strategy. Its three main elements were as follows:

1. Full review of existing formalities prior to including them in a central registry of all business formalities, with a guillotine rule by which any formality not contained in the registry was deemed automatically void.
2. Creation of an Economic Deregulation Council (CDE) to assist in the identification and review of relevant regulatory reform measures, supervise implementation by the ministries, and hold the UDE to

account with respect to its mandate. The government then went ahead to fully institutionalize the regulatory reform program and set its legal basis in law. It created COFEMER (*Comisión Federal de Mejora Regulatoria*), giving it full technical autonomy to design and implement regulatory reform policy in Mexico.

3. All regulatory proposals having business impacts, however small, had to be sent to the UDE for review, along with a technical justification of the measure. In addition, an amendment to the administrative procedures law was passed in 1996 to formally require RIAs in these cases. As such, most NTMs were subject to full UDE analysis and review before being submitted to COCEX for its opinion. The RIA requirement shifted the burden of proof to the ministries proposing regulation, which forced them to make their motivations more transparent. RIAs had to include the general public objectives of their proposals, an explanation of how the alternative proposed would be the least restrictive option, an estimation of costs and benefits, and a description of the resources that would be necessary for effective implementation. The UDE would then review this information and present recommendations to the ministry. If the recommendations were not accepted, the issue would be raised to the CDE to pressure the ministry into compliance. A key element of this process was that council members were all ministers or their equivalents, and it is obviously very costly for a minister in terms of time and reputation to appear recurrently before the CDE in order to defend questionable regulatory practices.

Phase 3: A new impetus to trade policy. More vibrant tariff liberalization was at the core of the most recent phase of trade reform in the last decade. Relatively high average most favored nation (MFN) tariffs and very low preferential FTA tariffs made Mexico's tariff structure very complex. This became a problem for many important manufacturing industries that depended on low cost inputs and machinery from non-FTA countries. Mexico also began to frequently impose antidumping measures, applying more than 90 countervailing duties, which affected nearly 1,400 tariff lines in 2002. The majority of these duties exceeded 200 percent and many were well over 500 percent (WTO 2002). With such a huge disparity in duties, the incentives to transship goods through the United States or to engage in other forms of contraband were significant. It was estimated that the amount of contraband goods sold in street markets in Mexico ranged from 50 to 90 percent for clothing, music, software, cigars, and footwear.

The government decided to proceed more vigorously with unilateral tariff liberalization starting in 2006. The first major step was to reduce MFN rates of over 6,000 tariff lines of inputs and raw materials (especially textiles, chemicals, and ore) relevant for 18 sectors in which tariff heterogeneity was high and where the cumulative tariff rates on inputs was higher than for the finished goods, which obviously reduced incentives to produce in Mexico. Then Mexico pushed the process of unilateral market opening further in 2008, based on a general reduction of MFN tariff levels, the simplification of exceptions and customs procedures, and the strengthening of COCEX's institutional design. Industrial MFN tariff levels dropped from 10.4 percent in 2008 to 5.3 percent in 2010 and are scheduled to reach 4.3 percent by 2013. The number of duty-free tariff lines was also increased from 20 percent in 2008 to 63 percent in 2010, the result being that over 90 percent of imports now enter Mexico duty-free. Finally, Mexico and China entered into an agreement in 2008 that obligated Mexico to repeal a large number of antidumping duties in areas such as textiles, apparel, footwear, toys, bicycles, tools, chemical products, valves, and locks, by 2011. To minimize opposition to the agreement, reconversion funds were approved by Congress.

Further simplification of trade regulations and procedures was also at the heart of this phase. Mexico took the pragmatic and brave decision to simplify its conformity assessment procedures by formally recognizing the equivalence between Canadian, United States, and Mexican safety standards for selected products, starting with household appliances and business electronic equipment (the government passed a decree that accepts certification of compliance with North American standards for commercialization of the products in Mexico). The same measure was taken for medical devices in October 2010 by COFEPRIS (*Comisión Federal para la Protección contra Riesgos Sanitarios*, Federal Commission for the Protection Against Sanitary Risks) to expedite access to safe and effective medical devices that comply with North American standards, an issue that had been raised in COFEMER recommendations since 2000. The government did not consult formally with the private sector through the usual COFEMER procedure, however. Indeed, the law allows for an exemption of RIA for rule changes that are judged to reduce compliance costs.

These decisions represent an important policy shift in practice, because traditionally the Mexican government had sought to promote harmonization (convergence of standards) or mutual recognition of conformity assessment procedures, rather than outright recognition of foreign certification (box 4.1). Laboratories and conformity assessment bodies were obviously against the measure, because equivalence eliminates the need

---

Box 4.1

Mexico Standards Modernization: The Case of Food Labeling

The 1996 mandatory technical standard on food labeling in Mexico was a contentious trade-related measure that had been the subject of much debate for the better part of 10 years. The standard mandates the labeling of nutritional content and consumer information for most packaged foods in Mexico, but it did not until recently conform to the international standard set by the by the UN's Codex Alimentarius Commission.[a] Foreign imports were subject to ex ante and sometimes discretional conformity assessment procedures at the border, where their products were sometimes immobilized for containing additional information or health claims not covered by the standard. Domestic interests were mostly content with the fact that the standard acted as a trade barrier that obstructed access to foreign goods. The government was dissatisfied with the fact that the regulation did not appear to be efficiently achieving its stated health goals. The complaints and defenses of the standard for the better part of a decade were generally unorganized and led to sterile discussions that did not produce any concrete outcomes.

Finally, in 2008, a number of factors came into play to push for the review of the standard that eventually led to its modification and harmonization with international standards. The first has to do with a COFEMER-sponsored reform to the Federal Standards and Metrology Law in 1997 that required a five-year review and automatic sunsetting clause of technical standards, and a default requirement of harmonization with international standards. Upon the date of the second five-year review date in 2008, importers made it clear that the standard was obsolete and out of line with international standards. The second major factor was that the government was pushing for a major campaign against obesity and wanted to ensure that the standard was generating useful consumer health information in line with government policy.

A review and RIA of the standard was initiated as a combined effort of the Economics Ministry and COFEPRIS. The first advantage of the RIA was that it clearly

(continued next page)

Box 4.1 *(continued)*

stated which issues were to be reviewed (consumer identification of health risks, clarification of information and health claims to be included in labels, harmonization with international standards, compliance costs, and conformity assessment procedures), which helped enormously in ordering the discussion. During the time where the regulatory process was opaque, the government had little incentive to confront protectionist interests, and the inefficient aspects of the standard were never really publicly debated. The mandatory public five-year review allowed parties interested in modifying the standard to be heard and to push for harmonization. Once the review process was opened, everyone had an equal opportunity to publicly present their views.

The RIA also shifted the debate toward a more technical discussion. The government was forced to present credible studies and data regarding the incidence and effects of health claims, and the importance of reliable nutritional information. It also began to present trade facilitation arguments as an additional benefit to consumers, thanks to the involvement of the trade unit of the Ministry of Economy. The business sector opposed to harmonization had to present reasonable arguments against changing the standards, and could no longer rely on directly lobbying the government on protectionist grounds. It focused, therefore, on the potential compliance costs of the regulatory change derived from the large inventories that would be "caught" in noncompliance. Importers presented information regarding the costs due to uncertainty of the rules themselves and the discriminatory nature of at-the-border inspections, rather than regular "retail shelf inspections."

Although the quality of the data presented was certainly not immune from criticism of bias, and one cannot say that the estimation of compliance costs was satisfactory, the mere presentation of legitimate issues rather than backdoor lobbying was enormously helpful in shaping the debate. Because the default position required by law is one of harmonization with international standards, the Codex standard was used as a model, and it proved impossible for opposing parties to discredit it or allege that domestic conditions in Mexico were different. The principles of harmonization and nondiscrimination of foreign products were agreed upon, and all that was left was to attend the stranded inventories argument. This issue was resolved by incorporating a gradual implementation of the new obligations over one full year. This was sufficient to overcome business and conformity assessment bodies' opposition to the changes and the new standard was published in February of 2010.

Source: Haddou 2012.

a. Codex was created in 1963 by the UN Food and Agriculture Organization and World Health Organization to develop food standards, guidelines, and related texts, such as codes of practice under the Joint FAO/WHO Food Standards Programme.

for Mexican certification for imports, but the gains from avoiding unnecessary delays and testing costs which negatively affected the availability of goods and prices for consumers sufficed to overcome domestic resistance.

Finally, the Mexican government took action to improve the business environment for traders by improving border management. Since most technical regulations are verified at the border, the Government recognized that this creates two significant problems. First, it implies a complicated coordination issue between Customs officials, responsible ministries, and private conformity assessment bodies, which can generate costs and delays. Second, these procedures may potentially be used as a way of containing imports in defense of certain products and industries. The proportion of tariff lines subject to border inspection of standards is as high as 70 to 90 percent in the case of food, textiles, and footwear.

COFEMER was actually one of the first institutions to point out the need for a detailed review of customs regulations and procedures to better meet the needs of export and import firms. In particular, it pointed to the increase in border crossing times and bureaucratic formalities that were beginning to seriously burden Mexico's trade competitiveness. For example, the growth of customs brokers, which hold a monopoly on the processing of foreign trade transactions, did not keep pace with the growth in trade volume in the 1990s, and has remained stable for the last decade. Moreover, the trade ministry was still handling foreign trade regulations and formalities with the same budget it had 10 years earlier.

On the customs administration side, the work with business associations has led to the elimination of the sectoral import registries, that is, the burdensome requirement of having to identify and label individual units of goods at the border, and the posting of bonds in the case of goods that were subject to estimated pricing rules. A one-stop shop project for customs and foreign trade regulation—similar in design to the SARE[2] (*Sistema de Apertura Rapida de Empresas*)—is also being implemented. The regulations of all ministries that need to be enforced by customs authorities will be included in a single portal for foreign trade formalities, and direct access will be granted to the private sector (not only customs brokers, but also trade advisors and shipping companies).

Rules of origin requirements are now more uniform. Negotiations for the accumulation of rules of origin in textiles for Mexico and Central American nations, as well as with the Dominican Republic and the United States, have been concluded to support the competitiveness of the textile industry at the regional level and of Mexican exports in particular. The agreements make it easier for producers to draw on the participating countries for their supplies at preferential tariff levels, thereby allowing the finished products to acquire originating status.

Lessons learned from Mexican regulatory reform

- **Trade policy reform should be comprehensive and coherent.** Mexico pursued trade competitiveness through different and complementary angles. It reduced tariffs unilaterally but also with a number of important partners. It upgraded its trade legal framework through the adoption of various laws to secure a transparent and fair trade. It aimed at facilitating import and export procedures through a regulatory review but also a simplification of border procedures and recognition of conformity assessments from its largest trading partners, the United States and Canada.

- **Making trade competitiveness a central piece of business regulatory review.** Mexico's experience illustrates the importance of including trade issues under the fold of a government-wide regulatory improvement program. Transparency, public comment, and technical justification are needed in the case of trade related measures, just as for any other sort of regulation. RIA of NTMs and regulatory proposals in general should be applied both ex ante and ex post to ensure proper design; to correct assessment of benefits and cost (effects not only on government revenue, but also on the volume of trade, consumers, business competitiveness, employment, competition, and social objectives); and to quickly identify ways of improving the regulatory environment.

- **Coordination and evaluation of trade policy and its regulation.** A central body should be entrusted with the overall design and implementation of policy, and the coordination of all of the different agencies involved. The goal should be to reach consensus with regard to the objectives and use of instruments of trade policy, and to periodically and transparently evaluate its effectiveness with respect to pre-established parameters. This would help in conferring a clear common vision to trade policy and to reduce the occurrence of ad hoc regulatory reactions to protectionist pressures and special interests.

Mauritius

Mauritius has embarked on an ambitious competitiveness agenda to achieve its *Vision 2020* blueprints written in the mid-1990s. The objective was to reorient the Mauritian economy from a labor-intensive model that had reached the limits of development and to respond to the triple trade shock that deteriorated its terms of trade (loss of sugar and textile preferences and soaring oil prices). Mauritius envisioned becoming a more competitive, innovative, and knowledge- and skill-based economy, creating more value-added jobs and increasing per capita levels. However, the first policy measures relied on picking winners—providing special incentives and targeted public investments—and have not delivered the expected results. A more comprehensive agenda was called for and legitimated by the 2005 elections. The new agenda included a number of cross-cutting measures that addressed inefficiencies in the investment, incentive, and labor regimes. It also aimed at improving competitiveness of firms by reducing and then eliminating tariffs to become a duty-free island.

Emergence of the NTM agenda: Developing procedures. With the reduction in tariffs, non-tariff barriers (NTBs) emerged as a clear obstacle dampening the competitiveness of the domestic economy (see box 4.2 for examples). Compliance with foreign NTBs was also harming the country's competitiveness and integration with the world economy by holding back its export performance. When the benefits that would come from a systematic process for the review of regulations and their implementation became apparent, the government decided to undertake that effort. Following passage of the budget of June 2008[3] the Ministry of the Economy was given the task of reviewing all permits and licenses. The Permit Review Committee (PRC) was established to review the need for import/export permits where they existed and also to submit proposals for the simplified processes and procedures for the issue of such permits and clearances.

The PRC conducted 13 meetings and consultations to carry out its mandate. First it identified a number of tariff lines requiring permits/clearances from various ministries and organizations and requested each ministry to submit the necessary justifications for maintaining permits under their purview. The PRC also requested all players to submit the detailed procedures, fees payable, and processing time for the issuance of permits, as well as the relevant related legislation. As a result of this exercise, the PRC identified about 19 types of permits that were affecting trade—issued mainly by six ministries, affecting almost a quarter of the tariff lines (2,610 out of 6,298 tariff lines)—for reasons of consumer protection, safety, phytosanitary standards, compliance to norms or standards, or compliance to international agreements. The necessity for these import/export permits was found unnecessary or unwarranted in 72 instances.

Box 4.2

Two Regulations That Hurt the Competitiveness of Mauritian Firms

Regulation Designed without Reference to Impact and Capacity to Implement

Problem: The government has defined the public policy objective of shielding citizens from toxic chemicals. The relevant regulation, the Dangerous Drug Act, seeks to achieve this through a ban on the importation of a defined list of toxic chemicals. While it is straightforward to prevent the importation of these materials in bulk form, the capacity is lacking to inspect and test imports of final products containing toxic ingredients, such as paints.

   Impact: While Mauritian firms can no longer use the toxic chemicals, products containing toxic chemicals are still being sold on the domestic market. According to the Mauritius Paint Association, the production cost of paint produced in Mauritius has increased since the non-toxic ingredients that must now be used are more expensive. Thus Mauritian producers of paint find it more difficult to compete in the domestic market with imported paints that contain the toxic materials. They also are at a competitive disadvantage in export markets that have not banned such ingredients.

Plant Health Regulations Create Obstacles to Flower Exporters

Problem: Mauritius was a global market leader in traditional red anthurium flowers. International competitors have developed new species in various colors as a marketing tool. Local producers would like to respond by growing a wider range of varieties. There is a risk of bacterial infection from imported plants that could spread to domestic production. In response, the government has banned the import of adult plants regardless of the risk that the particular imports may contain the bacteria. The capacity is lacking to test plants for the presence of the bacteria, and the government currently does not accept certificates confirming that plants are disease free from foreign laboratories. This forces exporters to import only baby plants (which do not contain the bacteria) which take up to two years to grow enough to be sold on the market.

   Impact: Anthurium exporters claim that the import ban on adult plants has prevented them from following market trends and it has marginalized Mauritius as a single variety exporter (see chapter 5 for a full case study).

The PRC also noted that some ministries or their departments experienced capacity constraints in terms of human resource or logistics, which greatly hampered the delivery of timely services, thus unduly increasing the processing time. It was therefore recommended that, apart from streamlining the procedures and processes involved, permit-issuing bodies had to ensure that the relevant unit or section was adequately staffed and equipped. There was also to be a general shift in mindset with a focus on a high standard of service delivery and only essential control exercised.

In addition to this important identification step, the World Bank (Brenton, Jensen, and Malouche 2009) has recommended the government take this effort to the next step in order to further streamline the regulations by accomplishing the following:

• Set up a permanent regulatory review committee. The committee would have the responsibility to (1) define the general principles of regulatory reform based on international best practice and to ensure that these are applied consistently across government; (2) review all new and important existing regulations; (3) oversee the introduction of RIA as a key tool across the government; and (4) facilitate the inter-ministerial coordination that is essential to address a wide range of the regulatory constraints, including duplication of requirements, that currently undermine competitiveness in Mauritius.
• Introduce an appeal mechanism to allow affected stakeholders the opportunity to contest the decisions of civil servants that they feel are incorrect, unfair, or arbitrary.[5]
• Assess capacity gaps that undermine effectiveness and efficiency of implementation. There are clearly critical gaps in the standards and conformity assessment infrastructure that need to be identified and prioritized in terms of the needs of business and the effectiveness of regulations.

A broader business regulatory review. The streamlining of Mauritius's permits and licenses soon showed its limitations when it came to trade regulations. A diagnostic of the trade regulations revealed a number of cases that deserved a deeper regulatory analysis (see Brenton, Jensen, and Malouche 2009) and weaknesses in the regulatory system in Mauritius that were undermining competitiveness, including the following:

• **Lack of systematic approach to assessment of regulations and their implementation.** There was no clear procedure by which actual and proposed regulations were examined and analyzed in terms of whether the design was consistent (1) with the underlying public policy objective; (2) with the capacity in government ministries and agencies and in the private sector to effectively implement them; and (3) in terms of impacts on competitiveness, growth, employment, and poverty.

- **Lack of transparency in design and application of regulations.** Regulations were not designed on the basis of consultation with interested stakeholders, even with different parts of the government.

- **Resources were poorly utilized due to lack of risk-based approach in many parts of the government.** With the exception of customs, most government ministries and agencies took a very rigid approach to the implementation of regulations and did not apply risk-based approaches that targeted resources, such as those for inspection, at the most risky transactions. Hence, for example, firms and individuals that invested in processes and procedures that reduce risks faced similar compliance costs to those whose products or activities posed a greater risk. These high compliance costs and the lack of flexibility inhibited international competitiveness relative to countries where the regulatory system and its application encourage rather than stifle innovation.

- **No recourse to dispute procedures was in place.** Individuals and firms had no formal mechanism by which to challenge the decisions of civil servants as they implement regulations. In practice, large firms and well connected individuals are able to exert influence and obtain a review of decisions that they deem to be incorrect or inappropriate. It is small and new firms and ordinary individuals who are unable to dispute decisions.

- **Duplication of requirements across government ministries and agencies.** In many cases, different parts of the government were making similar requirements, such as permits or licenses or the testing of products, to achieve the same objective. For example, the export of fish requires permits from the Ministry of Fisheries and the Ministry of Agriculture to achieve essentially the same purpose of monitoring and collecting information—information recorded by Customs and readily available. This also reflected the lack of coordination and cooperation across ministries and agencies. While different groups of the government have responsibility for achieving the same public policy objective, the efficiency in achieving this objective was often undermined by lack of coordination and cooperation.

- **Lack of competitiveness perspective in many ministries and agencies.** The culmination of the above weaknesses was that in designing and implementing regulations, few ministries or agencies considered the impact of their actions on the country's competitiveness. The World Bank recommended an approach similar to trade facilitation in Customs, be spread throughout the government, leading to a move from a rigid, non-contestable mindset in which ministries and agencies sought to shelter their requirements and approaches to one in which civil servants are continually exploring ways in which to better design and implement regulations through openness and cooperation.

Recognizing the need to carry out rigorous regulatory review for NTMs, the Government of Mauritius established a public-private review committee for NTBs chaired by the Ministry of Foreign Trade in April 2009 to (1) define the general principles of regulatory reform across government, (2) review all new and important existing regulations, (3) oversee the introduction of regulatory impact analysis as a key tool across the government, (4) facilitate coordination among ministries, and (5) encourage and assist the rollout of information technology solutions for trade facilitation across ministries and agencies.

While establishment of the review committee generated productive dialogue among various agencies and the private sector and helped identify various cases requiring government attention, the committee was unable to address the issues because of lack of human and technical capabilities dedicated to this process. Given the government's continued commitment to remove barriers to trade, it further strengthened the business regulatory review mechanism in early 2012 by establishing a joint public-private business facilitation task force to coordinate and strengthen the review process for business regulations and procedures, including a committee dedicated to the review of NTMs. This new task force will bring together the programs of four existing subcommittees dealing with business regulations, including the NTB Review Committee. It also put in place a secretariat, with administrative and technical staff and a dedicated budget, to make sure regulatory impact assessments would be conducted when needed.

In addition, with the assistance of the World Bank, two pilot regulatory impact assessments were conducted on the two cases presented in box 4.2, which helped interested parties in the government and private sector to analyze these problems and formulate measures to resolve them (see cases studies in chapter 5).

Indonesia

Indonesia has embarked on the most ambitious reform program in the Association of Southeast Asian Nations (ASEAN) under the leadership of its Ministry of Trade. The drive for reform comes in part from recognizing that, despite healthy growth rates, Indonesia is finding it difficult to expand and modernize its manufacturing base at a sufficient pace to generate the jobs it needs. Starting in 2004 the government implemented a series of reforms to lower tariffs, improve trade facilitation, and design measures to improve the regulatory environment for private investment.

Indonesia initiated a unilateral tariff harmonization program in 2005 that not only lowered the average MFN tariff rate, from 9.9 percent in 2004 to 7.5 percent in 2010, but also reduced tariff dispersion and tariff peaks. In 2009 the government also launched the Indonesia National Single Window (INSW), an integrated on-line clearance process for trade in goods, in major ports as a response to the regional call for better trade facilitation. In the investment arena, the government introduced a negative list of investments that provide national treatment to foreign investors in the context of the 2005 investment law. Despite its implication for limiting foreign equity participation, this negative list provides transparency for investors where private investment is still regulated across economic sectors.

As tariff rates went down, Indonesia faced a new challenge in rationalizing the use of NTMs. Such use, notably import licenses and control, increased since 2002 during which Ministries of Industry and Trade were merged into one. In recent years, lists of a "new generation" of NTMs—such as sanitary and phytosanitary (SPS) labeling, and technical standards—have been introduced for certain public policy objectives. Taking into account SPS and import restrictions on dangerous goods, current NTMs cover about 42 percent of Indonesia's 8,750 import tariff lines. Although most of the measures are for legitimate reasons, the process by which those measures are implemented is both cumbersome and in conflict with the idea of better trade facilitation under INSW. Meanwhile there has been anecdotal evidence that new NTMs were issued to satisfy protectionist calls from domestic industries, for example, an import prohibition on salt, certification of certain steel products, and certain technical standards that are not compatible with international standards.

NTMs in Indonesia have also evolved into different types, reflecting changes in pressure from domestic industries and growing needs of a more modern society. NTMs can be grouped in three main types: (1) Import licensing and registration, which cover various licenses related to imports, with permits and registration issued by the Ministry of Trade and licenses issued by the National Agency of Drug and Food Control (BPOM, *Badan Pengawas Obat dan Makanan*); (2) SPS related measures, mainly quarantine requirements for animals and plants; and (3) certification and technical standards, which require that products be certified or proven compliant with Indonesia's National Standard requirements. A few products also require certification from specific agencies, such as the Ministry of Communication or Ministry of Energy and Minerals.

There is also a group of "old-fashioned" types of NTMs: import ban, import quota, and trade by state-owned enterprises and the relatively new Customs preinspection requirement and port limitation for imports of certain products. Currently the most widely used of such NTMs is pre-shipment inspection (PSI). Figure 4.1 shows that 1,240 products are subject to PSI, surpassing the number of products that require importers

Figure 4.1   Numbers of Products Subject to NTMs in Indonesia

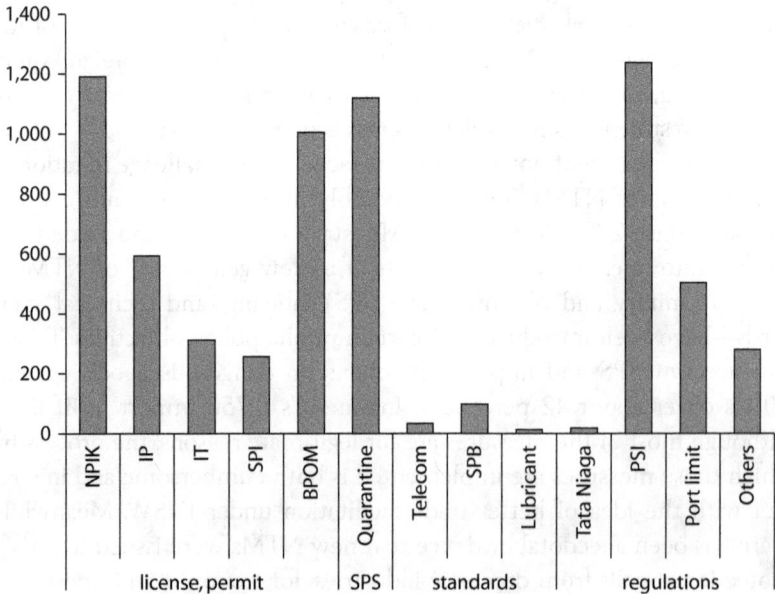

Source: LARTAS website.
Note: NPIK (*Nomor Pengenal Importir Khusus*) = Specific Importer Identification Number; IP (*Importir Produsen*) = Producer Importer License; IT (*Importir Terdaftar*) = Registered Importer License; SPI (*Surat Persetujuan Import*) = Import Approval Letter; BPOM (*Badan Pengawas Obat dan Makanan*) = National Agency of Drug and Food Control; SPB (*Surat Pendaftaran Barang*) = Commodity Registration Letter; PSI = pre-shipment inspection.

to obtain a Specific Importer Identification Number (NPIK). There are 1,195 products with 9-digit HS numbers that require NPIKs. The third most widely used type of NTM is import licenses issued by BPOM, which cover about 1,000 products.

With respect to issuing agencies, NTMs are no longer the main policy domain of the Ministry of Trade. Currently NTMs are issued by at least 13 different agencies (figure 4.2). The Ministry of Trade is responsible for issuing 61 percent of the total 6,677 NTMs. Meanwhile, Quarantine and BPOM are responsible for 17 and 15 percent of NTMs, respectively. Other ministries active in issuing NTMs are the Ministry of Health and Ministry of Agriculture.

Some imported products are subject to multiple NTMs; in fact, for several product groups, the total number of NTMs exceed the total number of tariff lines. Foodstuff has the highest number of NTMs per tariff lines. The second product group with the most NTMs is textiles and clothing. The intensive application of NTMs to certain products

Figure 4.2   NTMs Issued by Agency

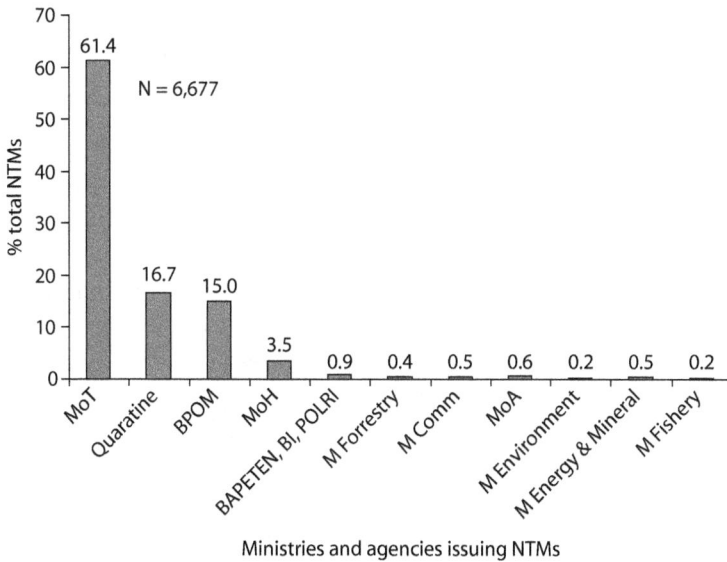

Ministries and agencies issuing NTMs

Source: LARTAS website.
Note: MoT = Ministry of Trade; BPOM = National Agency of Drug and Food Control; MoH = Ministry of Health; BAPETEN = Nuclear Energy Regulatory Agency; BI = Bank of Indonesia; POLRI = Police of Republic of Indonesia; M Comm = Ministry of Communication and Information; MoA = Ministry of Agriculture; M Environment = Ministry of Environment; M Energy & Mineral = Ministry of Energy and Mineral Resources; M Fishery = Ministry of Marine Affairs and Fisheries.

could suggest the government's initiative to closely monitor distribution of those products, but also may reflect the chain of regulations faced by for exporters and importers.

Government's response to NTM pervasiveness. The Indonesian government realized early on that reforming the NTM regime could help Indonesia internally and externally. On the defensive side, Indonesia could ensure that its NTMs are in compliance with different World Trade Organization (WTO) or ASEAN agreements. As the only developing country member from East Asia in the G20 process, Indonesia has committed to refrain from the use of protectionist instruments since the 2008–09 financial crisis began. Also, as signatories to the ASEAN Economic Community (AEC), Indonesia and other ASEAN countries have committed to identify and eliminate NTMs that are considered barriers by 2015 (more on regional initiatives in the next section). On the offensive side, reforming the NTM regime would increase economic productivity, which could help domestic industries in exploiting the gains from freer trade. The government addressed the NTM agenda through different mutually reinforcing lenses.

First, the government took an important step by enhancing the transparency of NTMs. Accessing information on Indonesia's NTMs was significantly improved after the Indonesia National Single Window (INSW) authority made them available online for importers and exporters.[5] As part of its mandate to integrate information for processing trade clearance, the agency put together an online database of Indonesian Import-Export Prohibition and Restriction Regulations (LARTAS database).[6]

Second, the government anchored the reforms to the regional commitment to operationalize the ASEAN Single Window by 2010. This has kick-started a slow process to rationalize trade regulations in Indonesia to achieve a well-functioning INSW. The process is quite complex because it requires strong coordination across a number of ministries. Almost all government agencies might issue a regulation that has an impact on trade, hence could be considered an NTM. It took about a year to get all agencies to list their trade-related regulations, then another year to put all the documents in a standard format, and another year to formulate the process for streamlining NTMs. Currently eight agencies are on board, representing 80 percent of the regulations.[7] Hence, the Coordinating Ministry of Economic Affairs, the coordinating agency for INSW, has become extremely important as the driver of an INSW forum in which users can share ideas on how to improve the INSW process, including implementation of NTMs.

Finally, the NTM reform process is receiving a new impetus, as the Ministry of Trade has just launched a pilot program establishing a review process for NTMs issued by this agency. A decree was adopted in September 2011 to create a review structure. The main thrust of the program is to remove the responsibility for reviewing NTMs from the unit that implements them and to equip the reviewing unit with adequate capacity to conduct regulatory impact analysis. The Directorate of Foreign Trade will continue to implement NTMs, while the unit that will review NTMs will be a "technical unit" composed of staff from various units but managed by the Trade Policy Research Unit. Both units will be part of a "non-tariff team" of the Ministry of Trade. The technical unit will be equipped with adequate capacity to conduct regulatory impact assessment for NTMs. To support the process, the Ministry would also introduce a standard operating procedure for reviewing NTMs.

Indonesia offers a model of transparency in the area of NTMs, having independently pioneered the NTM data collection process that is now under way around the world under the aegis of United Nations Conference on Trade and Development (UNCTAD), the World Bank, and other development agencies. Most interestingly, Indonesia's model of self-driven data collection and publication is based on an original incentive-compatible mechanism, under which customs pledges to enforce only those regulations that appear on the NTM inventory posted by the INSW. This overcomes a major difficulty encountered in other countries, where agencies issuing trade-restricting regulations resist exposing them to public scrutiny, preferring to keep them in semi-obscurity and providing them to importers at will.

Indonesian officials attribute this success to three main factors:[8] (1) a "champion ministry," which was the Ministry of Trade leading the effort with the support of the Ministry of Finance and the Coordinating Ministry for Economic Affairs; (2) an external deadline (ASEAN Single Window), reinforced by presidential directive, which helped the process move forward; and (3) identification of "quick winners," NTMs that would have immediate results, such as extending time for goods clearance to 24 hours a day, 7 days a week. The government is now planning a National Logistics System (logistics from end to end) to improve internal connectivity and the flow of goods. The government needs to develop a multi-modal transportation system to make movement of goods efficient across the 17,000 islands that make up the country.

Reforms Anchored in Regional Integration

In most regional agreements members commit to facilitate intraregional trade beyond tariff reduction and through the elimination of NTMs. Regional agreements provide a good opportunity for countries to simplify norms and standards, as well as to coordinate border clearance procedures for the internal circulation of goods. However, similar stated objectives by regional secretariats have led to various forms and levels of implementation of these commitments, which mostly depend on the political economy, capacity of national and regional institutions, and the approach adopted.

Among the factors that can challenge the process of improving NTMs is the political commitment of member countries to spur intraregional trade. Multiple free trade agreements (FTAs) among Arab countries, particularly those of the Maghreb, have led to little effective progress because of political tensions among members, Algeria, Libya, and Morocco. Similarly, the South Asia FTA is hampered by Pakistan-India political tensions. Such tensions limit the capacity of regional trade bodies which may have the mandate for a regional reform agenda but end up with little means and power to effectively lead the process. Another challenge comes from discrepancies in the capacity of national institutions, such as regulatory institutions, Customs administrations, and the standards bodies, in terms of human capital, equipment, and resources. These discrepancies have important consequences because they limit the potential for adopting mutual recognition of norms and standards or conformity assessments that would reduce the procedural burden among trading partners. Large investments may also be required to upgrade the trade facilitation infrastructure, and hence alleviate NTMs associated with these facilities.

Despite these challenges, some regions have been more successful than others in effectively addressing and streamlining NTMs. ASEAN has adopted the most ambitious NTM agenda among developing countries. Low-income economies in Southern Africa, also determined to address NTMs regionally, have achieved effective results in terms of transparency. Finally, the EU offers the most comprehensive example of economic integration of NTMs.

Association of Southeast Asian Nations

ASEAN members have implemented a number of measures that aim to rationalize tariffs and NTMs as part of their regional trade agenda.

Member countries adopted the new ASEAN harmonized tariff nomenclature at the customs level in 2002, and they harmonized to international standards TBTs dealing with consumer health and safety for 20 priority products in 2003, as well as standards for electrical safety in 2004. ASEAN also implemented a strategy for defeating NTMs, including a roadmap to eliminate trade-restrictive NTMs by 2010, later changed to 2015 for the ASEAN6 (Brunei Darussalam, Indonesia, Malaysia, the Philippines, Singapore, and Thailand), and 2018 for Cambodia, the Lao People's Democratic Republic Myanmar, and Vietnam.

The approach adopted by the ASEAN Secretariat was to classify NTMs in broad classes using several criteria. NTMs were first classified on the basis of the WTO principles regarding NTMs: measures are transparent, measures do not discriminate, SPS measures have a scientific basis, and whether there is no better, less trade-restrictive alternative (table 4.1). Moreover, the policy objectives and implementing procedures of these NTMs were identified. The Secretariat specifically took into account non-trade regulatory objectives, such as revenue generation and protection of health and safety of consumers. Finally, the Secretariat introduced the concept of "Trade Impact Criterion" to estimate the relative effects of a given NTM on welfare.

However, given the difficulties of quantifying the welfare impact of NTMs, more practical alternatives have been considered, including number of private sector complaints, difference between domestic and world prices, sectoral importance, and trade value. These criteria are not mutually exclusive and can be used singly or in combinations to set priorities. Based on the above criteria, NTMs were grouped into the following categories: (1) Red Box: NTMs impeding trade in ASEAN that require immediate elimination; (2) Amber Box: NTMs that could not be clearly identified or classified as barriers; and (3) Green Box: NTMs that could be justified, including measures that have a scientific basis and are applied to both domestic and imported goods.

The first step in the streamlining strategy was to eliminate NTMs that are potentially non-transparent and discriminatory in application, and next to eliminate NTMs that are transparent but discriminatory. NTMs deemed unnecessary would be removed without being replaced with alternative measures (for example, automatic licensing). For NTMs whose objective is protection, a reexamination is suggested in view of ASEAN members' commitment to promoting intraregional trade. In such case, the replacement of NTMs with tariffs should also be set, initially at rates with equivalent impact to the NTM, and gradually reduced in order

Table 4.1 NTM Classification Following WTO Consistency Criteria

Type of NTM by UNCTAD Code	Objective	Potential for nontransparent and discriminatory application	Scientific basis	Alternative measure that can achieve objective in less distortive manner
1400 –Tariff quota duties	Protection	None, since they are based on predetermined criteria, such as product type and amount, but discriminate between products	None	Tariffs
2200 – Additional charges	Revenue	None, since they are transparent and applied uniformly on imports	None	Uniform tax on both domestic and imported products
2300 – Internal taxes and charges levied on imports	Revenue or to cover administrative costs	None, since they are transparent and applied uniformly on imports	None	Uniform tax on both domestic and imported products
3100 – Administrative pricing	Protection through price control	Nontransparent basis for price; discriminates between products	None	Tariffs
3400 – Antidumping measures	Protection through price control	None, since they are transparent, covered by WTO Agreement	None	Remedy already provided under WTO rules
4300 – Restrictive official foreign exchange allocation	Control outflow of foreign exchange	Transparent but may discriminate between importers	None	Uniform surcharge on imports, or tax on all foreign exchange transactions, or some other form of capital control
5100 – Automatic licensing	Monitor imports	None, since they are freely granted	None	Ex-post reporting of imports based on customs entries
6100 – Non- automatic licensing	Protection through quantity control	Can be nontransparent, unpredictable, arbitrary, and/or discriminatory	None	Tariffs
6200 – Quotas	Protection through quantity control	Basis for quota may be non-transparent; discriminates between products	None	Tariffs

6300 – Prohibitions	Protection through quantity control; also for public health and safety, security, environmental, religious, moral reasons	Transparent but discriminates between products	Cover sensitive products, to protect health, safety, morals, security, environment	First establish that prohibition is not related to an SPS measure; tariffs if rationale is protection; domestic tax or regulation of consumption regardless of source if for technical reasons
6700 – Enterprise-specific restrictions	Selective protection	Procedures and their application can be non-transparent and discriminate between products	None	Tariffs; fiscal incentives given to selected sectors
7100 – Single channel for imports	Fiscal, economic, or social	Transparent but discriminates between products	None	Tax if fiscal; incentives if economic; tax or controls on domestic consumption or operation of buffer stock if social
8100 – Technical regulations	Protect health, safety, environment, security	Transparent administration and equal application on domestic and imported products is likely; however, they discriminate against subjected products	Yes for health, safety, environment or security reasons	At national level, comply with standards in Codex, IPPC, and IOE; at regional level, harmonization and mutual recognition of standards as in the EU and, to a lesser extent, the ASEAN
8200 – Pre-shipment inspection	Protect government revenue	Basis for quality, quantity, or price evaluation can be nontransparent; it discriminates between products and origins unless comprehensive	None	Risk management at Customs with post-entry audit
Customs and administrative procedures (rules of origin)	Prevent transshipment	Usually multiple and complex, but non-discriminatory	Ambiguous	Simplify multiple PSRO and use a uniform criterion across broad category of sectors

Source: Carrère, Céline, and de Melo 2009, adapted from de Dios 2004 and World Bank 2008.

Notes: UNCTAD Coding System of Trade Control Measures. Codex = Codex Alimentarius Commission. IPPC = International Plant Protection Convention. IOE = Industrial and Operating Engineering. PSRO = Product-Specific Rules of Origin.

to be less discriminatory against imports. Moreover, any less trade-distorting measure replacing an existing NTM would need to take into account the regulatory objectives of the original measures.

The ASEAN Secretariat determined that the greatest positive impact on trade is likely to come from removing the following NTMS: administrative pricing, non-automatic licensing, quotas, enterprise-specific restrictions, and pre-shipment inspection. These should be replaced with tariffs, fiscal incentives, or risk management with post-entry audit systems at customs. NTMs that are transparent but discriminate between imports should next be considered, although their immediate removal would also yield trade benefits (for example, prohibitions on "non-sensitive" goods and a single channel for imports).

The ASEAN Secretariat also sought to remove NTMs in nine priority sectors, including electrical equipment, organic chemicals, motor vehicles, pharmaceuticals, cosmetics, beverages, edible fruit and nuts, cocoa, and dairy products. Tariff quota duties, antidumping measures, and restrictive foreign exchange allocations were not included in the ASEAN scheme, because the last two affect products outside of the nine priority sectors, while antidumping is covered by WTO rules. Tariff quota duties may be converted into tariffs. Prohibitions are usually imposed on sensitive goods for national security, religious or moral, health and safety, or environmental reasons; hence those covering "non-sensitive" goods should be tackled first.

On the compliance side, the ASEAN Secretariat considered that enforcement of the rules may take place at different levels. Self-compliance is highly likely where the net benefits of the proposed arrangement are unequivocal for the member, which would serve as the impetus to implementation. Second- or third-party enforcement will require bodies with clear mandates, rules that are flexible yet stable, and quality information, but even more importantly, members' political will to deliver on their commitments. Nevertheless, formal mechanisms and arrangements within ASEAN were considered essential to institution-building because they improve on informal practices as well as instill a sense of obligation to the agreement by bringing countries under the same jurisdiction.

Nevertheless, the regionwide elimination of NTMs has been moving slowly, mainly because of difficult measurement and methodological issues. This reflects a challenge that many regional groups are facing when it comes to revamping NTMs. Pursuing the "elimination" of NTMs in the same way as tariffs may actually not be feasible. Instead, governments should aim at harmonizing or streamlining NTMs to reduce bureaucratic procedure and reduce compliance cost to trade with member countries. Acknowledging the lack of progress on the NTM agenda, the ASEAN Secretariat convened in July 2011 to seek agreement on baseline and objective indicators. This process was expected to better frame the regional efforts to streamline NTMs.

NTMs in Southern Africa

Regional integration efforts in Southern Africa, such as the Common Market for Eastern and Southern Africa (COMESA), Southern African Development Community (SADC), and Southern African Customs Union (SACU), have all sought to liberalize trade between countries in order to increase bilateral trade flows, diversify exports by overcoming the limits of small markets, and deepen specialization by achieving economies of scale.

Yet, despite these efforts, regional trade in Southern Africa has remained low because of trade barriers, particularly non-tariff barriers (NTBs), that persist at the regional level. The impact of these barriers on firms is pervasive. In a recent firm survey, which included five SADC countries, roughly 80 percent of respondents indicated that they faced some form of trade barrier within the region (RTFP 2009). Over half of the respondents indicated that the cost of these was equivalent to 5 percent of the cost, insurance, and freight value of their imports and exports. A further 24 percent of respondents indicated a 5–15 percent attribution to trade barriers, and 23 percent faced increased trade costs of over 15 percent.

There is also evidence that barriers in one form or another exist in all countries throughout the region. In an inventory of NTBs in SADC (RTFP 2007), all countries were found to maintain at least "moderate" barriers. These barriers are extremely costly, as illustrated in Gillson and Charalambides 2012. A plethora of barriers, such as trade permits, export taxes, import licenses, and bans, persists. Lack of coordination across government ministries and regulatory authorities also causes significant delays, particularly in authorizing trade for new products.

The commitment of Southern African countries to remove NTBs has focused so far on raising awareness and improving transparency, through identification and monitoring of NTBs. All agreements include clauses to eliminate NTBs. Article 6 of the SADC Trade Protocol calls for the elimination of all existing forms of NTBs and for member states to refrain from imposing new ones. While implementing this article remains a major challenge, SADC Ministers of Trade have identified ten categories of NTBs for "immediate" action: (1) cumbersome customs documentation and procedures, (2) cumbersome import and export licensing/permits, (3) import and export quotas, (4) unnecessary import bans and prohibitions, (5) import charges not falling within the definition of import duties, (6) restrictive single channel marketing, (7) prohibitive transit charges, (8) complicated visa requirements, (9) pre-shipment inspection, and (10) national food security restrictions. In some of these areas there has been progress, but in most, barriers still remain.

Most of the tangible efforts have focused on improving the monitoring and reporting of NTBs rather than eliminating them. Monitoring has taken two main forms:

- Audits on the implementation of the SADC Protocol on Trade have been undertaken every year since 2007. Their main focus has been on progress in removing tariffs facing regional trade, as per countries' commitments, but they also review some NTBs, in particular those relating to rules of origin.
- An SADC Trade Monitoring and Compliance Mechanism (TMCM) was established in mid-2008. It has two distinct elements: an online NTB Monitoring Mechanism (NTBMM) that records reported NTBs by firms and the aim of elimination and reduction of barriers (both tariffs and NTBs) following bilateral negotiation or outcomes from the various dispute settlement mechanisms.

The publication of NTBs under the auspices of the NTBMM is a major step forward. However, while the NTBMM is now well established (see box 4.3), it still has problems such as misidentification of some of the

Box 4.3

The Tripartite NTB Monitoring Mechanism

Shared by SADC, COMESA, and the East African Community, the NTBMM is a web-based "post box" where the private sector can report complaints against NTBs to regional trade in Southern and Eastern Africa. So far under the NTBMM, 335 complaints of NTBs have been made against barriers originating in 20 countries. The greatest number of complaints have been made by Namibia (66), followed by

(continued on next page)

Box 4.3 *(continued)*

South Africa (46), Zimbabwe (39), and Malawi (30). The three most cited countries for imposing NTBs are South Africa (40 cases), Namibia (36), and Malawi (33). An assessment of the types of barriers cited in the NTBMM and the number of complaints in each category is shown in table B4.3.1. Trade-related administrative barriers are reported most frequently by firms as an impediment to regional trade, followed by import licensing.

Table B4.3.1   NTBs Cited in the NTBMM

Barrier	No. of complaints
Trade-related administrative NTBs	74
Export and import licenses	39
Transit issues	36
Technical barriers to trade	32
SPS measures	28
Rules of origin	26
Clearance procedures	24
Quotas	19
Payments	21
Customs documentation	17
Pre-shipment inspection	8
Customs valuation	6
Immigration requirements for cross-border traders	4
Safeguards	1

Source: Charalambides (2010).

barriers reported and, most importantly, slow progress in resolving the barriers once they have been notified. Just half of the complaints received by SADC and 20 percent received by COMESA have been resolved under the Tripartite Monitoring Mechanism. The main reason is because there is no obligation for countries to remove their barriers once notified by others; enforcement relies purely on moral suasion.

NTMs in the European Union

The "Single Market" achieved by EU economic integration presents the most comprehensive program to reduce the incidence of NTBs in the internal single market. It is based on three principles: (1) non-discrimination, (2) mutual recognition, and (3) community legislation to ensure the functioning of the common market. The so-called four "freedoms" that cover the movement for goods, persons, services, and capital are the result of the abolition of customs duties, quantitative restrictions (QRs), and measures having equivalent effect to customs duties and QRs. Measures having equivalent effect are defined by the European Court of Justice: "All trading rules enacted by Member States which are capable of hindering, directly or indirectly, actually or potentially, intra-Community trade are considered as having an effect equivalent to QRs." Some 16 measures have been identified as having equivalent effects.

The European Commission also prohibits all types of trade remedies that include anti-dumping, safeguards, and countervailing measures. In addition, under "Mutual Recognition," a member state may not prohibit the sale of goods lawfully produced in another member state. This was illustrated in the 1979 Cassis de Dijon case, in which an importer was prohibited by the German authorities from importing Cassis de Dijon, a French liqueur, into Germany, on the grounds that its alcoholic strength was too low. The European Court of Justice held that the measure was equivalent to a quota, because it would have the practical effect of restricting imports, even though it did not directly target imported goods.

New law (harmonized legislation) was adopted when existing rules, mostly on health, safety, or environmental protection, differed too much across members, and starting in 1985, physical barriers (border checks and customs formalities) were eliminated.

The Single Action Plan was adopted in 1997 to speed up the necessary integration of the Single Market with a scoreboard of implementation enacted mainly to address slow progress in some areas that had equivalent effects, like public sector purchases of non-domestic origin. The Single Action Plan also dealt with formal infringement procedures. If a country fails to comply after the procedure, the European Court of Justice has the power to impose penalty payments and take away privileges of the trader from the country as a last resort.

The EU also developed and applied the principle of mutual recognition in standards that facilitate free intra-EU trade in goods. For example, alcoholic beverages can now be introduced into any other EU member state when they have been lawfully produced and marketed in one of the member states. This streamlined approach to intra-EU trade relies only on "essential requirements" of alcoholic beverages and provides greater freedom to manufacturers to fulfill those requirements.

More recently, Central European Free Trade Agreement (CEFTA) members that aim to join the EU have committed to eliminate NTMs with the EU. The fact that all countries in the region are adopting

European standards means that their systems are converging, which in the long-run will eliminate TBTs in the bloc (see box 4.4).

However, despite the substantive progress by CEFTA members, most countries are still lagging behind in converging toward the EU *acquis* in this area; thus, full alignment (and convergence) requires intensified and sustained efforts in this complex area. Croatia is, expectedly, most advanced in transforming its quality infrastructure; it has adopted most European Standards (ENs) and has a relatively well developed infrastructure with over 140 conformity assessment bodies. Albania and Bosnia and Herzegovina have also adopted substantial shares of ENs (mostly by endorsement). According to the European Commission, despite the various degrees of progress, all countries need to further align their legislation in the area of free movement of goods with the EU *acquis*. In many of the countries, the institutional set-up is well in place, but administrative capacities need to be strengthened to ensure proper implementation and enforcement.

The CEFTA Agreement introduces several novelties that aim to limit the use of SPS measures as a barrier to trade. SPS measures are regulated in chapter III on agriculture products, and article 12 of the Agreement obliges all parties to apply the WTO Agreement on the application of SPS

Box 4.4

CEFTA and TBTs

TBTs are regulated in chapter IV of the CEFTA Agreement, which obliges all parties to apply the WTO Agreement on TBTs. Article 13 requires that "the parties undertake to identify and eliminate unnecessary existing technical barriers to trade within the meaning of the WTO Agreement on TBTs." In addition, the Parties are required to "undertake not to introduce new unnecessary technical barriers to trade" and "shall inform...of any draft text for a new technical regulation or standard." Moreover, "the Parties are strongly encouraged...to harmonize their technical regulations, standards and procedures for assessment of conformity with those in the European Community." The Agreement specifies a concrete deadline for action on this issue, requiring that: "the Parties undertake to enter into negotiations to conclude plurilateral agreements on harmonization of their technical regulations and standards, and the mutual recognition of conformity assessment procedures...before 31 December 2010."

Source: Handjiski et al. (2010).

measures. The same article requires that "the Parties shall co-operate in the field of sanitary and phytosanitary measures, including veterinary matters, with the aim of applying relevant regulations in a nondiscriminatory manner." In addition, it obliges parties to provide information on SPS measures upon request of another party. Moreover, "The Parties shall enter, where appropriate, into negotiations to conclude agreements on harmonization or mutual recognition in threes matters..." The collaboration on these matters is fostered by the CEFTA Subcommittee on NTBs.

However, since the agreement entered into force, firms from several South East Europe countries have complained about cases of SPS measures being used as a barrier to trade. Moreover, several countries have introduced measures (of SPS nature) that limit or prohibit imports from other CEFTA parties. Some of these have been resolved within the CEFTA framework, but others continue to be applied. For example, Croatia, Former Yugoslav Republic of Macedonia, and Serbia have bans on import of some Change to "meat" products (some of these bans precede the CEFTA Agreement). The business communities in Bosnia and Herzegovina and Montenegro have complained that excessive inspection procedures and sampling of certain food products constitute discriminatory SPS measures.

Conclusion. Reforms that achieve the most effective results are those driven unilaterally by governments that seek to drastically improve domestic business competitiveness and integrate their countries' trade into the world economy. Regional agreements also offer an opportunity for economies to facilitate trade with selected member countries, including by streamlining NTMs through harmonization of standards and regulations, mutual recognition of conformity assessments, and reduction of border procedures. While all regional agreements include commitments to eliminate NTMs, effective results have been hard to achieve.

Notes

1. Following Mexico's 1982 financial crisis, Mexican output drifted down for nearly 2 years before rising again and did not recover to pre-crisis levels for 5 years. Although Mexican economic output dropped more quickly in 1995, it also rebounded more quickly, reaching pre-crisis peaks by the end of 1996. Similarly, following the 1982 crisis, it took Mexico 7 years to return to international capital markets, while in 1995, it took 7 months.

2. System for rapid business opening created by COFEMER, which led to the improvement in Doing Business Rankings.

3. The 2008–09 Government of Mauritius Budget Speech said: "We also want to significantly simplify the processes for exports and imports where bureaucracy can be unnecessarily exasperating in many cases. Our aim is to reduce the number of permits relating to imports and exports to the essential minimum, by 1st July 2009. Provisions will therefore be made under the Customs Act to suspend as from 1 July 2009 all permits relating to imports and exports, except those that are considered essential. All permit authorities will have until end December 2008 to submit to a Committee chaired by the Ministry of Business, Enterprise and Cooperatives, any justifications for maintaining the permits they issue. Furthermore, the Committee will recommend measures to lower compliances costs."

4. One approach used in other countries is to establish an ombudsman's office. Best practices have been defined by the International Ombudsman Association at http://www.ombudsassociation.org/standards.

5. The INSW automated system integrates the flow of data in different agencies into a single portal. The system allows users to simultaneously submit applications for export or import clearance to different agencies. To make the process transparent, the INSW authority set up an online database to pool information from different agencies about qualifications for obtaining Customs clearance for different products, and nontariff measures.

6. LARTAS means prohibition and limitation and has been terminology for Customs on requirements and regulations prior to the clearance of goods from ports.

7. These agencies are Ministry of Trade, Quarantine (Animal Quarantine, Fisheries Quarantine, and Plant Quarantine), Ministry of Transportation, BPOM (Food and Drug Agency), Nuclear Energy Regulatory Agency, and Customs.

8. Information provided by the Minister of Trade at a conference on trade facilitation organized by the World Bank, May 6, 2010, in Washington, DC.

References

Brenton, Paul, Michael Jensen, and Mariem Malouche. 2009. "The Trade Regulatory Framework for a Dynamic Global Competitor: The Case for Reform in Mauritius." Unpublished document, World Bank, Washington, DC.

Carrère, Céline, and J. de Melo. 2009. "Non-Tariff Measures: What Do We Know, What Should Be Done ?" Unpublished manuscript, World Bank, Washington, DC.

Charalambides, N. 2010. "Addressing NTBs in Regional Goods Trade in Southern African Countries." Sustainable Commerce Consulting, Gaborone, Botswana.

De Dios, Lorelei Cataylo. 2004. "Issues and Options for the Work Programme to Eliminate NTBs in AFTA." IBF International Consulting in association with Crown Agents and CSIS.

Gillson, Ian, and Nick Charalambides. 2012. Addressing Non-Tariff Barriers on Regional Trade in Southern Africa, In *Non-Tariff Measures—A Fresh Look at Trade Policy's New Frontier*, ed. Olivier Cadot and Mariem Malouche. London/ Washington, DC: Centre for Economic Policy Research/World Bank.

Haddou, A. 2012. "Streamlining of Non-tariff Measures in Mexico." In *Non-Tariff Measures—A Fresh Look at Trade Policy's New Frontier*, ed. Olivier Cadot and Mariem Malouche. London/Washington, DC: Centre for Economic Policy Research/World Bank.

Handjiski, Borko, Robert Lucas, Philip Martin, and Selen Sarisoy Guerin. 2010. "Enhancing Regional Trade Integration in Southeast Europe." World Bank Working Paper 185, World Bank, Washington, DC.

IQOM (Inteligencia Comercial) and Ernesto López Córdova. 2010. "Mexican Unilateral Trade Liberalization in the Middle of the Economic Crisis." Unpublished document.

RTFP (Regional Trade Facilitation Programme). 2007. "Inventory of Regional Non-tariff Barriers: Synthesis Report." RTFP, Pretoria, South Africa.

———. 2009. "Non-tariff Barrier Impact Study for COMESA Region." RTFP, Pretoria, South Africa.

World Bank. 2008. "Non-Tariff Measures on Goods Trade in the East African Community: Synthesis Report." Report No. 45708-AFR, World Bank, Washington, DC.

WTO (World Trade Organization). 2002, Trade Policy Review for Mexico: Secretariat Report. http://www.wto.org/english/tratop_e/tpr_e/tp190_e.htm.

CHAPTER 5

Streamlining NTMs: Case Studies

The case-by-case, consultative and analytical approach used in this toolkit was tested in three World Bank pilot case studies. In Mauritius, the case studies involved two regulations deadlocked between the government and the private sector: the import ban on adult anthurium plants, which the private sector claims has severely damaged the country's anthurium exports, and the ban on toxic paint pigments, which paint producers and exporters argue hurt export competitiveness in Southern African due to lack of regulation of the final product. In Nigeria, the case study assesses the cost of prohibiting import of 27 products and the effects on welfare and poverty. These case studies helped refine the qualitative information and issues that policy makers and analysts should review, as prescribed in the questionnaire on reviewing non-tariff measures (NTMs) (see appendix C). It also illustrates the quantitative analyses they should carry out when assessing the relevance and impact of NTMs, as discussed in chapter 2.

An SPS Measure: Import Ban and Environmental Protection

The Mauritius 2006 Plant Protection Act prohibits the import of adult anthurium plants that could possibly carry the anthurium blight bacterium. In the United Nations Conference on Trade and Development (UNCTAD) NTM classification, this falls under category A190, "prohibitions or restrictions for SPS reasons." Anthuriums (HS 06031090 at the 8-digit level; part of category HS 060310, "cut flowers and flower buds" at the 6-digit level) are grown in Mauritius and elsewhere for their beautiful, colorful, heart-shaped flowers. They are especially popular in Mauritius whose climate is favorable to their growth. However, they are under threat from a bacterium that causes the plant to wilt and die.

The initial symptoms of the "bacterial blight" disease—oily-looking leaf spots that turn yellow and become necrotic—can spread quickly through rainwater, wind, and human and animal contact, including to other species. There is no cure, and the blight bacteria remain in the environment. In the 1990s, the disease spread to almost all anthurium-producing countries, including Europe and Hawaii, and Mauritius's neighbor Reunion Island, where it was introduced by plants imported from Europe intended to be grown and re-exported, and it wrought havoc on the local industry. Only Mauritius was spared, thanks to a prompt ban on imports of adult plants. In order to maintain the island's pest-free status, the Mauritius Ministry of Agro Industry and Food Security allows only the import of baby plants grown in vitro, which are guaranteed pest-free by Dutch producers. Just to be sure, in-vitro baby plants are quarantined for 6 to 9 months, and 2 percent of them are tested for the bacterium. None has ever tested positive.

The ministry claims that this arsenal of measures is necessary to protect the environment and to protect producers from hurting themselves and the whole sector. Indeed, the measure easily passes the standards tests for review of NTMs—market failure and WTO-consistency.

Regarding the market failure test, the bacterium spreads to the environment, creating a potentially serious externality from anthurium producers to society at large, and even between producers themselves. An infected plant imported by one producer can easily contaminate others. An outbreak of the disease would likely mean the immediate destruction of all plants and capital (including the greenhouses themselves) by sanitary authorities, as was done in nearby Reunion. Subsequent production would entail drastic precautions, including decontamination of workers, mandatory use of disinfected equipment, and so on. Such precautions would be costly, especially for small farmers. Thus, one importer's mistake can entail enormously heavy costs for everyone—a classic case of externality.

As for WTO-consistency, the WTO SPS agreements mandate that any import-restricting measure be science-based. In the case of anthurium, scientific evidence on anthurium blight is beyond doubt, so the measure satisfies the basic requirements of the WTO's SPS agreement.

In addition, damage resulting from loose regulation would be largely irreversible. In the presence of large and irreversible risks, additional flexibilities are allowed by Article 5.2 of the WTO SPS agreement which allows countries to use the precautionary principle to impose measures, even in cases where scientific evidence is ambiguous (which is not the case here).

Industry representatives complain that the ban is responsible for the decline of Mauritius's anthurium exports, which were the world's first. Indeed, figure 5.1 shows that the country's exports of cut flowers have declined continuously since the mid-1990s.

The key issue in the private sector's argument is the causation from the regulation to the decline of the industry. According to industry representatives, imported in-vitro plants must be nurtured for up to two years (including the quarantine period) before being productive. This means a substantial immobilization of capital, although the quarantine period is partly subsidized by the state (the fee charged does not recover costs). Moreover, in a fashion-driven industry like cut flowers, where color nuances constantly change, reactivity is key. A two-year delay between ordering the baby plant from Holland and delivering the flowers to EU buyers can be problematic, although all producers are subject to the same constraint, one way or another.

A closer examination of figure 5.1 suggests that the decline in Mauritius's anthurium exports started in 1995, right after a hurricane hit

Figure 5.1   Decline in Mauritius Exports of Cut Flowers (HS 060310)

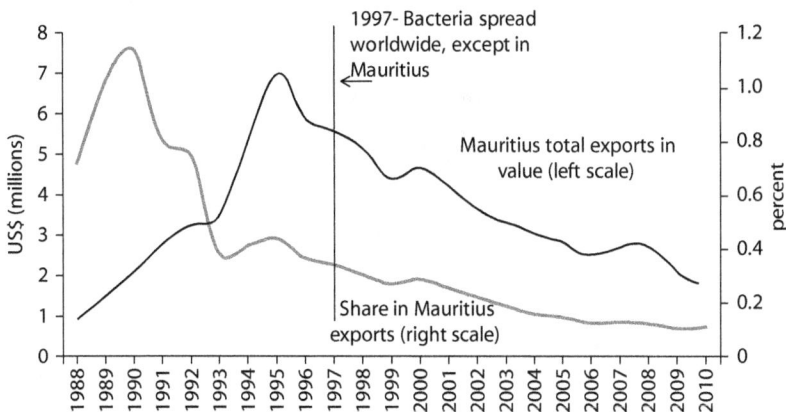

Source: UN Comtrade data and authors' calculation.

the island and destroyed large chunks of plant capital. The slow decline that followed suggests that the hurricane was not the only force at play, but it also suggests that the ban on adult plant imports was not the only one either. Indeed, interviews with producers suggest a nuanced picture with multiple factors affected the decline.

Does Mauritius have a comparative advantage in anthurium production? On the basis of endowments alone, the answer is yes, given its favorable climate. But it is unclear whether other factors make it possible to leverage this latent comparative advantage into competitive advantage in world markets. Anthurium flowers fetch a high unit price, which makes it suitable for air freight, but relative to other flowers, it is relatively heavy and bulky, which puts Mauritian producers at a disadvantage, given the high cost of air freight from the island. In addition, Mauritius exports to the EU market are of relatively limited quantities and it has failed to position itself clearly in a high-end segment sheltered from cut-throat competition from Chinese and other producers. As a result, many of the island's small producers are caught in a segment whose demand comes essentially from Italian buyers during festive periods. This market is difficult and fraught with moral hazard, including non-payment of shipments by importers.

Assessing precisely how much the ban actually contributed to the industry's decline would require an in-depth study that goes beyond the toolkit's application. It is also unnecessary—letting bygones be bygones. Today, after more than 15 years of decline, total industry employment is down to about 250 workers, and producers themselves acknowledge that lifting the ban alone would do little to trigger re-entry into the industry. The return to capital has become so low relative to alternative investment opportunities, in particular in non-tradable sectors, that it does not cover the opportunity cost of land. In other words, if a hurricane were to hit tomorrow, few if any would return to anthurium production.

Industry representatives surveyed for this case study estimate the annual loss of sales due to the ban at $450,000. They also estimate the cost of a disease outbreak for the industry at $22.9 million. In addition, it needs to be determined whether the risk created by a relaxation of phytosanitary controls would extend to the environment and biodiversity, creating a negative externality. As part of the application of the toolkit, an expert opinion was solicited from a biologist at the University of Mauritius. Excerpts from her report are reproduced in box 5.1. As it turns out, the expert opinion suggests that risks for the environment at large are minimal, so the cost-benefit calculation can be based on costs to the producers themselves only. Note that it is nevertheless an externality—a "market failure" justifying government intervention—if the actions of one importer can generate a loss for the entire industry.

Applying the technique to determine price gap and welfare outlined in appendix D, with a discount rate of 7 percent, a probability of infection

---

Box 5.1

Risks to the Environment: A Biologist's Expert Opinion

Bacteria in the environment are usually harbored in plant hosts; so plants in which the microorganism is detected must be destroyed to prevent any spread of bacteria. From the available scientific reports, the strains of *X. axonopodis pv. dieffenbachiae* that are virulent on anthuriums, are also quite effective on other plants, therefore, there is a low risk of it spreading uncontrollably in the environment. Healthy anthuriums could be infected by transfer of the bacteria from other infected plants nearby or through irrigation from an infected area to a clean one. If the bacterium were to show up in Mauritius, its anthurium plantations would likely suffer major losses. All plants would have to be destroyed and replaced with healthy ones, which would then have to be closely monitored by sensitive detection methods. The damage would be mainly to the anthurium sector, although other ornamentals might also be affected. The only way to reverse this damage would be to destroy all diseased plants as it is unlikely that the bacterium would survive long on non-host plants or in the soil.

Importing an adult plant can be risky if it comes from a region where the bacterium is present and where disease management measures are not well established and implemented. There is a low probability of the imported plant having the disease if it is from a country that does not have it. Phytosanitary certificates should be provided by the supplier before importing. Upon arrival in Mauritius, the plants should be screened by applying a well-designed sampling procedure and testing using the most sensitive methods, such as polymerase chain reaction (PCR), which can detect latent infections. There is a lower probability that in vitro plants will harbor the pathogen, although there are some reports of latent infection (low number of bacterial cells) from such plants. Notwithstanding the origin of import, monitoring should target latent infections, which would require molecular assays, the most sensitive method of detection, to be used.

Source: Biotechnology expert, University of Mauritius.

of 1/100,000 (producer's estimate), an inspection rate of 2 percent (indication from the Agro Industry Ministry), and imports of 6,875 plants per year,[1] the relevant magnitudes, using the notation of the appendix, are as follows:

PDV (present discounted value) of the prohibition's cost:

$$\frac{c}{1-\delta} = \$6.7 \text{ million}$$

Expected cost of lifting the prohibition

$$\frac{pL}{1-\delta(1-p)} = \$19.2 \text{ million}$$

Thus, taking into account only the cost of an outbreak of the bacterium to the industry itself—without regard to wider externalities to the environment—suggests that the expected cost of lifting the ban would outweigh the PDV of the cost of maintaining it. However, this estimate is very sensitive to the producers' estimate of the probability that any plant is infected. With a probability as low as 1/100,000, the Ministry of Agro Industry sampling scheme (testing 2 percent of the plants) is efficient in a particular sense: the probability of finding an infected plant on a small sample of 138 plants (2 percent of 6,875) is low, so the power of the test is low, but the probability of infection is also low, so the probability of an accident (an undetected infection) is contained at 6 percent—which may nevertheless be a high risk for society.

Should the probability of infection rise, the low power of the test would become costly. For instance, with an infection probability of 0.001 (one per thousand), the sample would still be too low for the test to be powerful, so the probability of an accident would rise to a whopping 87 percent. With the probability of infection rising still to 10 percent, however, the probability of accident (undetected infection) would shrink back down to almost zero, as even a small sample of 138 plants would be enough to catch at least one infected plant with quasi-certainty. In that case, the sampling would act like a de facto prohibition (since every shipment anyway would have at least one infected plant with such a high infection rate).

In conclusion, application of the toolkit suggests that even though the ban on imports of adult plants may have contributed to the decline of Mauritius's anthurium production and exports over the last 10–15 years, today the case for lifting the ban is not favorable in view of the limited benefits it would confer to an industry that suffers from many other competitive disadvantages and of the potential for irreversible damage to the environment and to whatever remains of the industry itself.

A TBT Measure and Incoherence along the Value Chain

Under Mauritius's 2004 Dangerous Chemicals Control Act the import of toxic paint pigments (red lead oxide and calcium plumbate) is prohibited. These products can be replaced by other, less toxic ones (titanium dioxide and zinc phosphate respectively). However, the substitutes are more expensive. Asked about the reasons for the ban, the Occupational Health Unit of the Ministry of Health and Quality of Life mentioned three concerns: (1) occupational health (handling of the banned chemicals involves health hazards for workers); (2) the environment (handling of the banned chemicals involves a risk of spill); and (3) consumer safety (the banned chemicals conserve their toxicity when embodied in paint). No prioritization of these concerns was offered.

Paint imports are covered by the Consumer Protection Act, which does not prohibit the import of paints manufactured using the two toxic pigments mentioned above. Industry representatives have alerted the authorities to the fact that this dual treatment creates "reverse discrimination" against domestic producers, by subjecting them to a regulation that is not applied to importers. In addition, Mauritius's regulation raises the cost of producing paint by anything between 2 percent and 40 percent, depending on the product, which may hamper domestic producers' competitiveness on markets—for example, in continental Africa—where other producers are subject to no regulation.

Basic checks—the existence of a market failure and the measure's consistency with the WTO's TBT Agreement—are easily verified. The chemicals in question are toxic, even when embodied in paint, while consumers are unlikely to be aware of the hazard. The scientific basis for restricting the extent to which this toxic product hits the market is perfectly sound, and indeed Mauritius's regulation is backed by World Health Organization (WHO) agreements.

Is there a problem with the regulation's design? The reverse discrimination problem is real. Discussion by the World Bank expert team with representatives of the Ministry of Health suggested that the identification of where the market failure lies (occupational health, environment, or consumption) was not entirely clear, and that the overall coherence of the array of health regulations affecting the value chain from chemical inputs to paints had not been clearly thought out through coordination between the agencies concerned. The regulation of paint sales, which is what matters if the market failure is at the consumption level, falls under the Consumer Protection Act, whose enforcement is under the purview of the Mauritius Standards Bureau (MSB), not the Health Ministry. But the MSB does not have the technical capabilities to test for the presence of the toxic pigments in paint. All it can control is the residual lead level.

The problem with the regulation's design is not in the market failure it addresses—which is real—but in its precise location and the adequacy of the regulation's design to that location. Rather than through a ban on imports of the toxic intermediates, consumer protection from residual levels of toxic pigments should be regulated by a ban on the sale of paints produced with those toxic intermediates, irrespective of whether the paint is domestically produced or imported. Regulating only imports or only domestic production would be discriminatory, that is, against importers in the first case and against domestic producers in the second. Verification should take place on both domestic sales and imports, and it requires either equipping the MSB with adequate testing equipment (which would, according to industry representatives, cost about $200,000) or else certifying foreign testing facilities.

As for the ban on imported toxic pigments, it should be maintained only if needed for occupational safety or environmental (local pollution) reasons. What standards Mauritian producers apply on their export sales is, arguably, an issue of corporate social responsibility that is beyond the competence of national authorities.

To conclude, application of the toolkit suggests that the regulation of toxic pigments used in the manufacture of paint can be easily redesigned in a way that would both improve its performance in addressing the market failure it is meant to address and reduce its costs to Mauritian producers. The redesign involves shifting the locus of restrictive regulation from *imports* of the *intermediate* product to *sales* of the *final* product.

Prohibition and Its Impact on Welfare

Until 2010—when this toolkit was applied on a pilot basis—Nigeria prohibited the import of 27 groups of products (listed in table 5.1). The prohibitions covered a fairly wide range of products, including

Table 5.1   Nigeria's Prohibited Imports

1	Live or dead birds (including frozen pultry)
2	Pork, beef, mutton, lamb, goat meat
3	Bird eggs
4	Vegetable oils and fats
5	Spaghetti/noodles
6	Fruit juices in retail packs
7	Water (beverages)
8	Bagged cement
9	Drugs
10	Waste pharmaceuticals
11	Finished soaps and detergent
12	Mosquito repellant coils, disinfectants, germicides
13	Sanitary plastic ware
14	Toothpicks
15	Retreaded and used tires
16	Corrugated paper and paper board
17	Toilet paper
18	Textile fabrics, including African prints, Georges, lace, embroidered
19	Carpets
20	Made-up garments
21	All types of footwear and bags
22	Hollow glass bottles
23	Used compressors, air conditioners, refrigerator/freezers
24	Used motor vehicles over 15 years old
25	Furniture
26	Certain electric generating items
27	Ball point pens
28	Telephone recharge cards

Source: Nigeria Customs Service.

"necessities," such as those under category 26 (which include exercise books and pencils) or 9 (which include common pain killers such as aspirin and paracetamol).

In general, import bans have the effect of raising the domestic price of the prohibited products to the point where domestic supply meets domestic demand. In the case of Nigeria, even under an import ban, unknown quantities were smuggled into the country via a porous border with Benin. Little was known about the quantities involved and the cost of smuggling, so that this "hidden import supply" could not be estimated directly. What was clear, however, was that smuggling was costly and could not completely fill the vacuum created by the import ban. Thus, quantities available on the Nigerian domestic market were restricted and prices were higher than they would have been without the ban. This ban had three effects on the country's economy:

- It raised the rents accruing to domestic producers (largely in quasi-monopoly situations).
- It raised the cost of living and reduced the welfare of domestic consumers.
- It raised government tariff revenue.

Price-gap calculations using Nairobi as a comparator city for Lagos[2] suggested the ad-valorem equivalents (AVE) shown in table 5.2. As expected, price gaps were systematically larger for banned products than for other products. For banned products, the simple average was a whopping 92 percent (upper cell in the last column). For non-banned products, it was 15 percent (lower cell in the last column). That left an average price gap of 67 percent for banned products, after controlling for cost-of-living differences.

Eliminating the bans would generate a real-income gain that could be "allocated" by income category using household expenditure patterns obtained from Nigeria's household survey. The result is shown in figure 5.2. Because the banned products account for a slightly larger share of the budget of low-income households (1st and 2nd quartiles), lifting the bans could be expected to have a pro-poor effect and to generate an overall real-income gain over 9 percent.

Plugging these results into the Nigerian Household Survey suggests that as many as 3 million Nigerians could be lifted out of poverty—that is, cross the poverty line—as a result of eliminating the ban, not accounting for employment effects. Of course, employment effects should be estimated in such a simulation, but no useable data could be obtained, even with the help of an ad-hoc survey carried out for that purpose by the World Bank's local office. Thus, the effect on employment resulted in only a conceptual argument—namely, that domestic

Table 5.2   Price Gap Calculations, Lagos vs. Nairobi (% of price gap)

	Staples	Protein	Beverages	Household supplies	Personal care products	Total
Banned products	178	30	−7	67	194	92
Other	61	−24	−26	−12	−17	15

Source: Economist Intelligence Unit; World Bank calculations.

Figure 5.2   Real-Income Gain from Eliminating Import Bans, by Income Level and Product Category

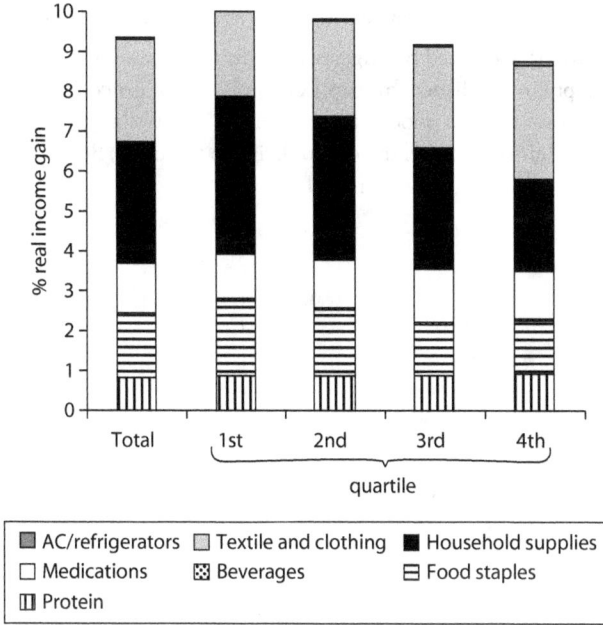

Source: World Bank calculations.

monopolies were unlikely to have experienced much expansion of employment as a result of the higher prices generated by the bans, because monopolies, unlike competitive firms, deliberately keep output and employment low when protected by trade measures in order to keep prices and margins high. Thus, domestic monopolies were unlikely to reduce employment by much as a result of elimination of the bans. In addition, whatever employment gains the bans generated accrued largely in the capital city, Lagos, as the cost of the ban in terms of higher prices was found to be higher in remote regions where the incidence of poverty was higher, reinforcing the idea of the bans' regressive (anti-poor) bias.

In conclusion, application of the toolkit suggests that eliminating the ban would generate substantial consumer gains that would be unlikely to be offset by employment losses, although the availability of data in Nigeria made it impossible to get a complete picture.

Notes

1. Mauritius Ministry of Agro-industry reckons that about 55,000 plants were imported over an eight-year period, or 6,875 per year on average.

2. For the products affected by Nigeria's prohibition phase-outs, the calculations used the prices published by the Economist Intelligence Unit (EIU) for a basket of consumption goods observed in the world's largest cities. The EIU provides no information on the cost of living in Cotonou, Benin, which would have been a natural comparator for Lagos.

UNCTAD NTM Classification, February 2012

A SANITARY AND PHYTOSANITARY MEASURES

Measures that are applied to protect human or animal life from risks arising from additives, contaminants, toxins or disease-causing organisms in their food; to protect human life from plant- or animal-carried diseases; to protect animal or plant life from pests, diseases, or disease-causing organisms; to prevent or limit other damage to a country from the entry, establishment or spread of pests; and to protect bio-diversity. These include measures taken to protect the health of fish and wild fauna, as well as of forests and wild flora.

Note that measures for environmental protection (other than as defined above), to protect consumer interests, or for the welfare of animals, are not covered by SPS.

Measures classified under A1 through A6 are Technical Regulations while those in A8 are their Conformity Assessment Procedures.

A1 Prohibitions/restrictions of imports for SPS reasons

Prohibition and/or restriction of the final products to be imported are classified in this chapter. Restrictions on the tolerance limits on residues or use of certain substances contained in the final products are classified under A2 below.

A11 Temporary geographic prohibitions for SPS reasons
Prohibition of imports of specified products from countries or regions due to infectious/contagious diseases: Measures included in this category are typically more of an ad-hoc and time-bound nature.
Example: Imports of poultry from areas affected by avian flu or cattle from foot and mouth disease affected countries are prohibited.

A12 Geographical restrictions on eligibility
Prohibition of imports of specified products from specific countries or regions due to lack of evidence of sufficient safety conditions to avoid sanitary and phytosanitary hazards: The restriction is imposed automatically until the country proves employment of satisfactory sanitary and phytosanitary measures to provide a certain level of protection against hazards that are considered acceptable. Eligible countries are included in a "positive list." Imports from other countries are prohibited. The list may include authorized production establishments within the eligible country.
Example: Imports of dairy products from countries that have not proven satisfactory sanitary conditions are prohibited.

A13 Systems approach
An approach that combines two or more independent SPS measures on same product: The combined measures can be composed of any number of inter-related measures as well as their conformity assessment requirements and are applied at all stages of production.
Example: An import program establishes a package of measures that specifies pest-free production location, pesticides to be used, harvesting techniques as well as post-harvest fumigation, combined with inspection requirement at entry point: Hazard Analysis and Critical Control Point (HACCP) requirements.

A14 Special authorization requirement for SPS reasons
A requirement that importer should receive authorization, permit, or approval from a relevant government agency of the destination country for SPS reasons: In order to obtain the authorization, importers may need to comply with other related regulations and conformity assessments.

Example: An import authorization from the Ministry of Health is required.

A15 **Registration requirements for importers**

The requirement that importers should be registered before they can import certain products: To register, importers may need to comply with certain requirements, provide documentation and pay registration fees.

Example: Importers of a certain food item need to be registered at the Ministry of Health.

A19 **Prohibitions/restrictions of imports for SPS reasons n.e.s. (not elsewhere specified)**

A2 **Tolerance limits for residues and restricted use of substances**

A21 **Tolerance limits for residues of or contamination by certain (non-microbiological) substances**

A measure that establishes a maximum residue limit (MRL) or "tolerance limit" of substances such as fertilizers, pesticides, and certain chemicals and metals in food and feed, which are used during their production process but are not their intended ingredients: It includes a permissible maximum level (ML) for non-microbiological contaminants. Measures related to microbiological contaminants are classified under A4 below.

Example: (a) MRL is established for insecticides, pesticides, heavy metals, veterinary drug residues; (b) POPs and chemicals generated during processing; (c) residues of "dithianon" in apples and hops.

A22 **Restricted use of certain substances in foods and feeds and their contact materials**

Restriction or prohibition on the use of certain substances contained in food and feed. It includes the restrictions on substances contained in the food-containers that might migrate to food.

Example: (a) Certain restrictions exist for food and feed additives used for coloring, preservation, or sweeteners; (b) For food containers made of polyvinyl chloride plastic, vinyl chloride monomer must not exceed 1 mg per kg.

A3 Labeling, marking, and packaging requirements
A31 Labeling requirements
Measures defining the information directly related to food safety, which should be provided to the consumer: Labeling is any written, electronic, or graphic communication on the consumer packaging or on a separate but associated label.

Example: (a) Labels that must specify the storage conditions such as "5 degree C maximum"; (b) potentially dangerous ingredients such as allergens, e.g., "contains honey not suitable for children under one year of age."

A32 Marking requirements
Measures defining the information directly related to food safety, which should be carried by the packaging of goods for transportation and/or distribution.

Example: Outside transport container must be marked with instructions, such as handling for perishable goods, refrigeration needs, or protection from direct sunlight, etc.

A33 Packaging requirements
Measures regulating the mode in which goods must be or cannot be packed, or defining the packaging materials to be used, which are directly related to food safety.

Example: Use of PVC films for food packaging is restricted.

A4 Hygienic requirements
Requirements related to food quality, composition, and safety, which are usually based on hygienic and good manufacturing practices (GMPs), recognized methods of analysis and sampling: The requirements may be applied on the final product (A41) or on the production processes (A42).

A41 Microbiological criteria of the final product
Statement of the microorganisms of concern and/or their toxins/metabolites and the reason for that concern, the analytical methods for their detection and/or quantification in the final product: Microbiological limits should take into consideration the risk associated with the microorganisms, and the conditions under which the food is expected to be handled and consumed. Microbiological limits should also take account of the likelihood of uneven distribution of

microorganisms in the food and the inherent variability of the analytical procedure.

Examples: Liquid eggs should be pasteurized or otherwise treated to destroy all viable Salmonella microorganisms.

A42 Hygienic practices during production

Requirements principally intended to give guidance on the establishment and application of microbiological criteria for foods at any point in the food chain from primary production to final consumption: The safety of foods is principally assured by control at the source, product design and process control, and the application of Good Hygienic Practices during production, processing (including labeling), handling, distribution, storage, sale, preparation, and use.

Examples: Milking equipment on the farm should be cleaned daily with a specified detergent.

A49 Hygienic requirements n.e.s.

A5 Treatment for elimination of plant and animal pests and disease-causing organisms in the final product (e.g., post-harvest treatment)

Various treatments that can be applied during production or as a post-production process, in order to eliminate plant and animal pests or disease-causing organisms in the final product.

A51 Cold/heat treatment

Requirement of cooling/heating of products below/above a certain temperature for a certain period of time to kill targeted pests, either prior to or upon arrival to the destination country: Specific facilities on land or ships are requested. Containers should be equipped properly to conduct cold/heat treatment and should be equipped with temperature sensors.

Example: Citrus fruits must undergo cold (disinfection) treatment to eliminate fruit flies.

A52 Irradiation

Requirement to kill or devitalize microorganisms, bacteria, viruses, or insects that might be present in food and feed products by using irradiated energy (ionizing radiation).

Example: This technology may be applied on meat products, fresh fruits, spices, and dried vegetable seasonings.

A53 Fumigation

A process of exposing insects, fungal spores, or other organisms to the fumes of a chemical at a lethal strength in an enclosed space for a given period of time: Fumigant is a chemical, which at a required temperature and pressure can exist in the gaseous state in sufficient concentration to be lethal to a given pest organism.

Example: Use of acetic acid is mandatory as post harvest fumigant to destroy fungal spores on peaches, nectarines, apricots, and cherries; methyl bromide for fumigating cut flowers and many other commodities.

A59 Treatment for elimination of plant and animal pests and disease-causing organisms in the final product n.e.s.

A6 Other requirements on production or post-production processes

Requirement on other (post-) production processes not classified above: It also excludes those specific measures under **A2: Tolerance limits for residues and restricted use of substances** (or its sub-categories).

A61 Plant growth processes

Requirements on how a plant should be grown in terms of conditions related to temperature, light, spacing between plants, water, oxygen, mineral nutrients, etc.

Example: Seeding rate and row spacing of soybean plants are specified to reduce the risk of frogeye leaf spots

A62 Animal raising or catching processes

Requirements on how an animal should be raised or caught because of SPS concerns.

Example: Cattle should not be fed with feeds containing offal of cows suspected of BSE (Bovine Spongiform Encephalopathy).

A63 Food and feed processing

Requirements on how food or feed production should take place in order to satisfy sanitary conditions on the final products.

Example: New equipment or machinery for handling or processing feed in or around an establishment producing animal feed shall not contain polychlorinated biphenyls (PCBs).

A64 **Storage and transport conditions**
Requirements on certain conditions under which food and feed, plants and animal should be stored and/or transported:
Example: Certain foodstuffs should be stored in a dry place, or below certain temperature.

A69 **Other requirements on production or post-production processes n.e.s**

A8 **Conformity assessment related to SPS**
Requirement for verification that a given SPS condition has been met: It could be achieved by one or combined forms of inspection and approval procedure, including procedures for sampling, testing and inspection, evaluation, verification and assurance of conformity, accreditation and approval, etc.

A81 **Product registration requirement**
Product registration requirement in the importing country
Example: Requirements and guidelines for the registration of a pesticide and its compounds, for minor crops/minor use, and the maximum residue limit. The measure may include provisions describing types of pest control products that are exempt from registration and procedures detailing the registration process, including provisions relating to distribution, import, sampling, and detention.

A82 **Testing requirement**
A requirement for products to be tested against a given regulation, such as MRL: It includes sampling requirements.
Example: A test on a sample of orange imports is required to check against the maximum residue level of pesticides.

A83 **Certification requirement**
Certification of conformity with a given regulation: required by the importing country but may be issued in the exporting or the importing country.
Example: Certificate of conformity for materials in contact with food (containers, papers, plastics, etc.) is required.

A84 **Inspection requirement**
Requirement for product inspection in the importing country: May be performed by public or private entities. It is similar to testing, but it does not include laboratory testing.

Example: Animals or plant parts must be inspected before entry is allowed.

A85 Traceability requirements
Disclosure requirement of information that allows following a product through the stages of production, processing and distribution.

A851 Origin of materials and parts
Disclosure of information on the origin of materials and parts used in the final product.
Example: For vegetables, disclosure of information on the location of the farm, name of the farmer, and fertilizers used, may be required.

A852 Processing history
Disclosure of information on all stages of production: may include their locations, processing methods, and/or equipment and materials used.
Example: For meat products, disclosure of information on their slaughter house, as well as food processing factory, may be required.

A853 Distribution and location of products after delivery
Disclosure of information on when and how the goods have been distributed from the time of their delivery to distributors until they reach the final consumer.
Example: For rice, disclosure of information on the location of its temporary storage facility may be required.

A859 Traceability requirements n.e.s.

A86 Quarantine requirement
Requirement to detain or isolate animals, plants, or their products on arrival at a port or place for a given period in order to prevent the spread of infectious or contagious disease, or contamination.
Example: Live dogs must be quarantined for two weeks before entry into the territory is authorized. Plants need to be quarantined to terminate or restrict the spread of harmful organisms.

A89 Conformity assessment related to SPS n.e.s.

A9 SPS measures n.e.s.

B TECHNICAL BARRIERS TO TRADE

Measures referring to technical regulations and procedures for assessment of conformity with technical regulations and standards, excluding measures covered by the SPS Agreement.

A "technical regulation" is a document which lays down product characteristics or their related processes and production methods, including the applicable administrative provisions, with which compliance is mandatory. It may also include or deal exclusively with terminology, symbols, packaging, marking, or labeling requirements as they apply to a product, process, or production method. A "conformity assessment procedure" is any procedure used, directly or indirectly, to determine that relevant requirements in technical regulations or standards are fulfilled; it may include, inter alia, procedures for sampling, testing and inspection; evaluation, verification, and assurance of conformity; registration, accreditation, and approval, as well as their combinations.

Measures classified under B1 through B7 are Technical Regulations, while those under B8 are their Conformity Assessment Procedures. Among the Technical Regulations, those in B4 are related to production processes, while others are applied directly on products.

B1 Prohibitions/restrictions of imports for objectives set out in the TBT agreement

Such prohibitions/restrictions may be established for reasons related, inter alia, to national security requirements; the prevention of deceptive practices; protection of human health or safety, animal or plant life or health, or the environment. Restrictions on the tolerance limits on residues or use of certain substances contained in the final products are classified under B2.

B11 Prohibition for TBT reasons

Import prohibition for reasons set out in B1.

Example: Imports are prohibited for hazardous substances, including explosives; certain toxic substances covered by the Basel Convention, such as aerosol sprays containing CFCs; a range of HCFCs and BFCs; halons; methyl chloroform; and carbon tetrachloride.

B14 Authorization requirement for TBT reasons

Requirement that the importer should receive authorization, permit, or approval from a relevant government agency of the destination country, for reasons such as national security, environmental protection etc.

Example: Imports must be authorized for drugs, waste and scrap, fire arms, etc.

B15 Registration requirement for importers for TBT reasons
Requirement that importers should be registered in order to import certain products: To register, importers need to comply with certain requirements, documentation, and registration fees. It also includes the registration of establishments producing certain products.

Example: Importers of "sensitive products" such as medicines, drugs, explosives, firearms, alcohol, cigarettes, game machines, etc., may be required to be registered in the importing country.

B19 Prohibitions/restrictions of imports for objectives set out in the TBT agreement n.e.s.

B2 Tolerance limits for residues and restricted use of substances

B21 Tolerance limits for residues of or contamination by certain substances
A measure that establishes a maximum level or "tolerance limit" of substances, which are used during their production process but are not their intended ingredients.

Example: Salt level in cement or sulphur level in gasoline, must be below a specified amount.

B22 Restricted use of certain substances
Restriction of the use of certain substances as components or material to prevent the risks arising from their use.

Example: (a) Restricted use of solvents in paints; (b) the maximum level of lead allowed in consumer paint.

B3 Labeling, marking, and packaging requirements

B31 Labeling requirements
Measures regulating the kind, color, and size of printing on packages and labels and defining the information that should be provided to the consumer: Labeling is any written, electronic, or graphic communication on the packaging, or on a separate but associated label, or on the product itself. It may include requirements on the official language to be used as well

as technical information on the product, such as voltage, components, instruction on use, safety and security advisories, etc.
Example: Refrigerators need to carry a label indicating their size, weight, as well as electricity consumption level.

B32 Marking requirements
Measures defining the information for transport and customs that the transport/distribution packaging of goods should carry.
Example: Handling or storage conditions according to type of product, typically signs such as "FRAGILE" or "THIS SIDE UP," etc. must be marked on the transport container.

B33 Packaging requirements
Measures regulating the mode in which goods must be or cannot be packed, and defining the packaging materials to be used.
Example: Palletized containers or special packages need to be used for the protection of sensitive or fragile products.

B4 Production or Post-Production requirements

B41 TBT regulations on production processes
Requirement on production processes not classified under SPS above: It also excludes those specific measures under *B2 Tolerance limits for residues and restricted use of substances* (or its sub-categories).
Example: Use of environmentally friendly equipment is mandatory.

B42 TBT regulations on transport and storage
Requirements on certain conditions under which products should be stored and/or transported.
Example: Medicines should be stored below a certain temperature.

B49 Production or post-production requirements n.e.s.

B6 Product identity requirement
Conditions to be satisfied in order to identify a product with a certain denomination (including biological or organic labels).
Example: In order for a product to be identified as "chocolate," it must contain a minimum of 30% cocoa.

B7 **Product quality or performance requirement**
Conditions to be satisfied in terms of performance (e.g., durability, hardness) or quality (e.g., content of defined ingredients)
Example: Door must resist certain minimum high temperature.

B8 **Conformity assessment related to TBT**
Requirement for verification that a given TBT requirement has been met: it could be achieved by one or combined forms of inspection and approval procedure, including procedures for sampling, testing and inspection, evaluation, verification and assurance of conformity, accreditation and approval, etc.

B81 **Product registration requirement**
Product registration requirement in the importing country.
Example: Only the registered drugs and medicine may be imported.

B82 **Testing requirement**
A requirement for products to be tested against a given regulation, such as performance level: It includes sampling requirement.
Example: A testing on a sample of motor vehicle imports is required against the required safety compliance and its equipment, etc.

B83 **Certification requirement**
Certification of conformity with a given regulation: required by the importing country but may be issued in the exporting or the importing country.
Example: Certificate of conformity for electric products is required.

B84 **Inspection requirement**
Requirement for product inspection in the importing country: may be performed by public or private entities. It is similar to testing, but it does not include laboratory testing.
Example: Textile and clothing imports must be inspected for size and materials used before entry is allowed.

B85 **Traceability information requirements**
Disclosure requirement of information that allows following a product through the stages of production, processing, and distribution.

B851 Origin of materials and parts

Disclosure of information on the origin of materials and parts used in the final product.

Example: Manufacturers of automobiles must keep the record of the origin of the original set of tires for each individual vehicle.

B852 Processing history

Disclosure of information on all stages of production: may include their locations, processing methods, and/or equipment and materials used.

Example: For wool apparel product, disclosure of information on the origin of the sheep, location of the textile factory, as well as the identity of the final apparel producer may be required.

B853 Distribution and location of products after delivery

Disclosure of information on when and/or how the goods have been distributed during any time after the production and before final consumption.

Example: Before placing imported cosmetic products on the EU market, the person responsible must indicate to the competent authority of the Member State where the products were initially imported, the address of the manufacturer, or the address of the importer.

B859 Traceability requirements n.e.s.

B89 Conformity assessment related to TBT n.e.s.

B9 TBT measures n.e.s.

C PRE-SHIPMENT INSPECTION AND OTHER FORMALITIES

C1 Pre-shipment inspection

Compulsory quality, quantity, and price control of goods prior to shipment from the exporting country, conducted by an independent inspecting agency mandated by the authorities of the importing country.

Example: A pre-shipment inspection of textile imports by a third party for verification of colors and types of materials is required.

C2 Direct consignment requirement
Requirement that goods must be shipped directly from the country of origin, without stopping at a third country
Example: Goods imported under a preferential scheme such as GSP must be shipped directly from the country of origin in order to satisfy the scheme's rules of origin condition. (i.e., to guarantee that the products have not been manipulated, substituted, or further processed in any third country of transit).

C3 Requirement to pass through specified port of customs
Obligation for imports to pass through a designated entry point and/or customs office for inspection, testing, etc.
Example: DVD players need to be cleared at a designated customs office for inspection.

C4 Import monitoring and surveillance requirements and other automatic licensing measures
Administrative measures which seek to monitor the import value or volume of specified products.
Example: Automatic import license is required as an administrative procedure for textile and apparel prior to importation.

C9 Other formalities n.e.s.

D CONTINGENT TRADE PROTECTIVE MEASURES
Measures implemented to counteract particular adverse effects of imports in the market of the importing country, including measures aimed at "unfair" foreign trade practices, contingent upon the fulfillment of certain procedural and substantive requirements.

D1 Antidumping measure
A border measure applied to imports of a product from an exporter, which imports are dumped and are causing injury to the domestic industry producing the like product, or to third countries' exporters of that product. Dumping takes place when a product is introduced into the commerce of an importing country at less than its normal value, generally where the export price of the product is less than the comparable price, in the ordinary course of trade, for the like product when destined for consumption in the exporting country. Anti-dumping measures may take the form of anti-dumping duties or of price undertakings by the exporting firms.

D11 Antidumping investigation

An investigation initiated and conducted either following a complaint by the domestic industry producing the like product or (in special circumstances) self-initiated by importing country authorities to determine whether dumping of a product is occurring and is injuring national producers (or a third country's exporters) of the like product. Provisional duties may be applied during the investigation.

Example: An antidumping investigation was initiated by the European Union in respect of imports of "steel wire rod" from Country A.

D12 Antidumping duty

A duty levied on imports of a particular good originating from a specific trading partner to offset injurious dumping found to exist via an investigation. Duty rates are generally enterprise-specific.

Example: An antidumping duty of 8.5 to 36.2% has been imposed on imports of "biodiesel products" from Country A.

D13 Price undertaking

An undertaking by an exporter to increase its export price (by not more than the amount of the dumping margin) to avoid the imposition of antidumping duties. Prices can be negotiated for this purpose, but only after a preliminary determination that dumped imports are causing injury.

Example: An antidumping case involving "Flat-Rolled Products of Grain Oriented Silicon-Electrical Steel" resulted in the manufacturer undertaking to raise its export price.

D2 Countervailing measure

A border measure applied to imports of a product to offset any direct or indirect subsidy granted by authorities in an exporting country where subsidized imports of that product from that country are causing injury to the domestic industry producing the like product in the importing country. Countervailing measures may take the form of countervailing duties or of undertakings by the exporting firms or by authorities of the subsidizing country.

D21 Countervailing investigation

An investigation initiated and conducted either following a complaint by the domestic industry producing the like product or (in special circumstances), self-initiated by the importing country authorities to determine whether the imported goods are subsidized and are causing injury to national producers of the like product.

Example: A countervailing investigation was initiated by Canada in respect of imports of "oil country tubular goods" from Country A.

D22 Countervailing duty

A duty levied on imports of a particular product to offset the subsidies granted by the exporting country on the production or trade of that product, where an investigation has found that the subsidized imports are causing injury to of the domestic industry producing the like product.

Example: A countervailing duty of 44.71% has been imposed by Mexico on imports of "dynamic random access memory (DRAM) semiconductors" from Country A.

D23 Undertaking

Either an undertaking by an exporter to increase its export price (by not more than the amount of the subsidy), or an undertaking by the authorities of the subsidizing country to eliminate or limit the subsidy or take other measures concerning its effects, to avoid the imposition of countervailing duties. Undertakings can be negotiated only after a preliminary determination that subsidized imports are causing injury.

Example: A countervailing duty investigation involving "palm oil and margarine for puff pastry" from Country A resulted in the government of Country A undertaking to fully eliminate the subsidy on that product.

D3 Safeguard measures

D31 General (multilateral) safeguard

A temporary border measure imposed on imports of a product to prevent or remedy serious injury caused by increased imports of that product and to facilitate adjustment. A country may take a "safeguard" action (i.e., temporarily suspend multilateral concessions) in respect of imports of a product from all sources where an investigation has established that increased imports of the product are causing or threatening to cause serious injury to the domestic industry that produces like or directly competitive products. Safeguard measures can take various forms, including increased duties, quantitative restrictions, and others (e.g., tariff-rate quotas, price-based measures, special levies, etc.).[1]

D311 Safeguard investigation

An investigation conducted by the importing country authorities to determine whether the goods in question are being imported in such increased quantities and under such conditions as to cause or threaten to cause serious injury to national producers of like or directly competitive products.

Example: Country A has initiated a safeguard investigation on imports of certain motorcycles.

D312 Safeguard duty

A temporary duty levied on imports of a particular product to prevent or remedy serious injury from increased imports (as established in an investigation) and to facilitate adjustment. Where the expected duration of the measure is more than one year, it must be progressively liberalized during the period of application.

Example: A safeguard duty of three years duration has been imposed on imports of "Gamma Ferric Oxide." The level will be 15% during the first year, 10% during the second year, and 5% during the third year.

D313 Safeguard quantitative restriction

A temporary quantitative restriction on imports of a particular product, to prevent or remedy serious injury from increased imports (as established in an investigation) and to facilitate adjustment. Rules apply regarding the overall level and the allocation of the quota. Where the expected duration of the measure is more than one year, it must be progressively liberalized during the period of application.

Example: A quantitative safeguard measure (quota) of three years duration has been implemented on imports of certain steel products. The total level will be 10,000 tons the first year, 15,000 tons the second year, and 22,000 tons the third year.

D314 Safeguard measure, other form

A safeguard measure in a form other than a duty or quantitative restriction (which could include measures combining duties and quantitative elements), applied to prevent or remedy serious injury from increased imports (as established in an investigation) and to facilitate adjustment. Where the expected duration of the measure is more than one year, it must be progressively liberalized during the period of application.

Example: A safeguard measure of two years duration is imposed on imports of dishwashers. During the first year, a safeguard measure of $US 50 per unit will be applied to all imported dishwashers with a CIF price below $US 500 per unit. During the second year, the safeguard measure will not apply to the first 20,000 units of imports, regardless of the prices of those units.

D32 Agricultural special safeguard

Agricultural special safeguard allows the imposition of an additional tariff in response to a surge in imports or a fall in import prices. The specific trigger levels for volume or price of imports are defined at the country level. In the case of the volume trigger, the additional duties only apply until the end of the year in question. In the case of price triggers, the additional duty is imposed on a shipment by shipment basis.

D321 Volume-based agricultural special safeguard

In this type of safeguard, an additional duty may be applied if the volume of imports of designated agricultural product exceeds a defined trigger quantity.

Example: An additional duty equal to one-third the current applied duty is applied to imports of milk when the volume of imports exceeds the trigger volume of 861 tonnes.

D322 Price-based agricultural special safeguard

In this type of safeguard, an additional duty may be applied if the import price of a designated agricultural product falls below defined trigger price.

Example: An additional duty of 2.79 Php/kg is applied to a shipment of frozen meat and offal of fowls of the species Gallus domesticus when the c.i.f. import price of that shipment is 20 per cent below the trigger price of 93 Php/kg.

D39 **Safeguard n.e.s.**
This category could include, e.g., special safeguard mechanisms applicable to imports of a product under regional trade arrangements, protocols of accession, or other agreements.

E NON-AUTOMATIC LICENSING, QUOTAS, PROHIBITIONS, AND QUANTITY CONTROL MEASURES OTHER THAN FOR SPS OR TBT REASONS

Control measures generally aimed at restraining the quantity of goods that can be imported, regardless of whether they come from different sources or one specific supplier. These measures can take the form of non-automatic licensing, fixing of a predetermined quota, or prohibitions.[2] All measures introduced for SPS and TBT reasons are classified in Chapters A and B above.

E1 **Non-automatic import licensing procedures other than authorizations for SPS or TBT reasons**
An import licensing procedure introduced, for reasons other than SPS or TBT requirements, where approval is not granted in all cases: the approval may either be granted on a discretionary basis or may require specific criteria to be met before it is granted.

E11 **Licensing for economic reasons**

E111 **Licensing procedure with no specific ex-ante criteria**
Licensing procedure where approval is granted at the discretion of the issuing authority: it may also be referred to as a discretionary license.
Example: Imports of textile products are subject to a discretionary license.

E112 **Licensing for specified use**
Licensing procedure where approval is granted only for imports of products to be used for pre-specified purpose: normally granted for use in operations generating anticipated benefit in important domains of the economy.
Example: License to import high-energy explosives is granted only if it is used for mining industry.

E113 **Licensing linked with local production**
Licensing only for imports of products with linkage to local production, including the local production

level of the same product, except for such licensing classified as trade-related investment measures. (See See I1–I3).
Example: License to import gasoline is granted only if domestic supply is insufficient.

E119 Licensing for economic reasons n.e.s.

E12 Licensing for non-economic reasons

E121 Licensing for religious, moral, or cultural reasons
Control of imports by license for religious, moral, or cultural reasons.
Example: Imports of alcoholic beverages are permitted only by hotels and restaurants.

E122 Licensing for political reasons
Control of imports by license for political reasons.
Example: Imports of all products from a given country is subject to import license.

E129 Licensing for non-economic reasons n.e.s.

E2 Quotas
Restriction of importation of specified products through the setting of a maximum quantity or value that is authorized for import. No imports are allowed beyond those maximums.

E21 Permanent quotas
Quotas of a permanent nature (i.e., they are applied throughout the year, without a known date of termination of the measure) where the importation can take place any time of the year.

E211 Global allocation
Permanent quotas where no condition is attached to the country of origin of the product.
Example: A quota of 100 tons of fish where the importation can take any time of the year, and there is no restriction on the country of origin of the product.

E212 Country allocation
Permanent quotas where a fixed volume or value of the product must originate in one or more countries.

Example: A quota of 100 tons of fish that can be imported any time of the year, but where 75 tons must originate in country A and 25 tons in country B.

E22   Seasonal quotas

Quotas of a permanent nature (i.e., they are applied every year, without a known date of termination of the measure), where the importation must take place during a given period of the year.

E221   Global allocation

Seasonal quotas where no condition is attached to the country of origin of the product.

Example: An annual quota of 300 tons of seaweed where the importation must take place between March and June, and there is no restriction on the country of origin of the product.

E222   Country allocation

Seasonal quotas where a fixed volume or value of the product must originate in one or more countries.

Example: An annual quota of 300 tons of seaweed where the importation must take place during winter, and 60 tons must originate in country A and 40 tons in country B.

E23   Temporary quotas

Quotas that are applied for on a temporary basis (e.g., they are only applied for one or two years), whether or not they are also seasonal in nature.

E231   Global allocation

Temporary quotas where no condition is attached to the country of origin of the product.

Example: An annual quota of 1000 tons of fish and fish meat that will only be applied for three years, where there is no restriction on the country of origin of the product.

E232   Country allocation

Temporary quotas where a fixed volume or value of the product must originate in one or more countries.

Example: An annual quota of 1000 tons of fish and fish meat that will only be applied for three years, where the imports must take place during summer and 700 tons must originate in country A, 200 tons must originate in country B, and the remainder can originate in any country.

E3 Prohibitions other than for SPS and TBT reasons

Prohibition on the importation of specific products for reasons other than SPS (A1) or TBT (B1) reasons.

E31 Prohibition for economic reasons

E311 Full prohibition (import ban)

Prohibition without any additional condition or qualification.

Example: Import of "motor vehicle with cylinder under 1500cc" is not allowed to encourage domestic production.

E312 Seasonal prohibition

Prohibition of imports during a given period of the year. This is usually applied to certain agricultural products while the domestic harvest is in abundance.

Example: Import of strawberries is not allowed from March to June each year.

E313 Temporary prohibition, including suspension of issuance of licenses

Prohibition set for a given fixed period of time unrelated to a specific season: it is usually for urgent matters not covered under the safeguard measures of *D613*, above.

Example: Import of certain fish is prohibited with immediate effect until the end of the current season.

E314 Prohibition of importation in bulk

Prohibition of importation in a large-volume container: importation is only authorized if the product is packed in a small retail container, which increases per unit cost of imports.

Example: Import of wine is allowed only in a bottle of 750ml or less.

E315 Prohibition of products infringing patents or other intellectual property rights

Prohibition of copies or imitations of patented or trademarked products.

Example: Import of imitation brand handbags is prohibited.

E316 Prohibition of used, repaired or remanufactured goods
Prohibition to import goods that are not new
Example: Prohibition to import used cars

E319 Prohibition for economic reasons n.e.s.

E32 Prohibition for non-economic reasons

E321 Prohibition for religious, moral, or cultural reasons
Prohibition of imports for religious, moral, or cultural reasons not established in technical regulations.
Example: Imports of books and magazines displaying pornographic pictures are prohibited.

E322 Prohibition for political reasons (embargo)
Prohibition of imports from a country or group of countries, applied for political reasons.
Example: Imports of all goods from Country A are prohibited in retaliation for that country's testing of nuclear bombs.

E329 Prohibition for non-economic reasons n.e.s.

E5 Export restraint arrangement
An arrangement by which an exporter agrees to limit exports in order to avoid imposition of restrictions by the importing country, such as quotas, raised tariffs, or any other import controls.[3] The arrangement may be concluded at either government or industry level.

E51 Voluntary export restraint arrangements (VERs)
Arrangements made by government or industry of an exporting country to "voluntarily" limit exports in order to avoid imposition of mandatory restrictions by the importing country. Typically, VERs are a result of requests made by the importing country to provide a measure of protection for its domestic businesses that produce substitute goods.

E511 Quota agreement
A VER agreement that establishes export quotas.
Example: A bilateral quota on export of "motor vehicles" from Country A to Country B was established to avoid sanction by the latter.

E512   Consultation agreement

A VER agreement that provides for consultation with a view to introducing restrictions (quotas) under certain circumstances.

Example: An agreement was reached to restrict export of cotton from Country C to Country D in case the volume of export exceeds $2 million tons in the previous month.

E513   Administrative co-operation agreement

A VER agreement that provides for administrative cooperation with a view to avoiding disruptions in bilateral trade.

Example: An agreement was reached between Country E and Country F to cooperate to prevent sudden surge of exports.

E59   Export restraint arrangements n.e.s.

E6   Tariff Rate Quotas (TRQs)

A system of multiple tariff rates applicable to a same product: the lower rates apply up to a certain value or volume of imports, and the higher rates are charged on imports which exceed this amount.

Example: Rice may be imported free of duty up to the first 100,000 tons, after which it is subject to a tariff rate of $1.5 per kg.

E61   WTO bound TRQs

TRQs (as described above) included in WTO schedules.

E611   Global allocation

WTO bound TRQs where no condition is attached to the country of origin of the product.

Example: A WTO TRQ provides for duty-free import of milk and cream up to 2,000 tonnes with no condition attached to the country of origin.

E612   Country allocation

WTO bound TRQs where a fixed volume or value of the product must originate in one or more countries.

Example: A WTO TRQ of 200,000 tons of poultry with an in-quota duty of 12% is available, and half of the quantity must originate from country A.

E62 Other TRQs

TRQs (as described above) included in other trade agreements.

E621 Global allocation

Non-WTO TRQs where no condition is attached to the country of origin of the product.

Example: A non-WTO TRQ is available for 40,000 tonnes of beef with no condition attached to the country of origin.

E622 Country allocation

Non-WTO bound TRQs where a fixed volume or value of the product must originate in one or more countries.

Example: Fresh bananas from country A can be imported duty-free up to 4,000 tonnes.

E9 Quantity control measures n.e.s.

F PRICE CONTROL MEASURES INCLUDING ADDITIONAL TAXES AND CHARGES

Measures implemented to control or affect the prices of imported goods in order to, inter alia, support the domestic price of certain products when the import prices of these goods are lower; establish the domestic price of certain products because of price fluctuation in domestic markets or price instability in a foreign market; or to increase or preserve tax revenue. This category also includes measures, other than tariffs measures, that increase the cost of imports in a similar manner, i.e., by fixed percentage or by a fixed amount: they are also known as para-tariff measures.

F1 Administrative measures affecting customs value

Setting of import prices by the authorities of the importing country by taking into account the domestic prices of the producer or consumer: it could take the form of establishing floor and ceiling price limits or reverting to determined international market values. There may be different price setting, such as minimum import prices or prices set according to a reference.

F11 Minimum import prices

Pre-established import price below which imports cannot take place.

Example: A minimum import price is established for fabric and apparel.

F12 **Reference prices**
Pre-established import price which authorities of the import-ing country use as reference to verify the price of imports.
Example: Reference prices for agricultural products are based on "farm-gate price," which is the net value of the product when it leaves the farm, after marketing costs have been subtracted.

F19 **Other administrative measures affecting the customs value n.e.s.**

F2 **Voluntary export price restraints (VEPRs)**
An arrangement in which the exporter agrees to keep the price of his goods above a certain level[4]: A VEPR process is initiated by the importing country and is thus considered as an import measure.
Example: Export price of videocassette tape is set higher in order to defuse trade friction with major importing countries.

F3 **Variable charges**
Taxes or levies aimed at bringing the market prices of imported products in line with the prices of corresponding domestic prod-ucts[5]: Primary commodities may be charged per total weight, while charges on processed foodstuffs can be levied in proportion to the primary product contents in the final product. These charges include the following:

F31 **Variable levies**
A tax or levy whose rate varies inversely with the price of imports: It is applied mainly to primary products. It may be called flexible import fee.
Example: A tariff rate on beef is set as "$100 per kg minus the price per kg of beef on the invoice."

F32 **Variable components**
A tax or levy whose rate includes an *ad valorem* component and a variable component: These charges are applied mainly to processed products where the variable part is applied on the primary products or ingredients included the final prod-uct. It may be called compensatory element.
Example: A tariff rate on sugar confectionary is set as "25% plus 25$ per kg of contained sugar minus the price per kg of sugar".

F39 **Variable charges n.e.s**

F4 Customs surcharges
An ad hoc tax levied solely on imported products in addition to customs tariff to raise fiscal revenues or to protect domestic industries.
Example: *Customs surcharge, surtax, or additional duty.*

F5 Seasonal duties
Duties applicable at certain times of the year, usually in connection with agricultural products.
Example: *Imports of "fresh perry pears, in bulk" from 1 August to 31 December may enter free of duty, while in other months, seasonal duties applied.*

F6 Additional taxes and charges levied in connection to services provided by the Government
Additional charges, which are levied on imported goods in addition to customs duties and surcharges and which have no internal equivalents[6]: They include the following:

F61 Custom inspection, processing and servicing fees

F62 Merchandise handling or storing fees

F63 Tax on foreign exchange transactions

F64 Stamp tax

F65 Import license fee

F66 Consular invoice fee

F67 Statistical tax

F68 Tax on transport facilities

F69 Additional charges n.e.s.

F7 Internal taxes and charges levied on imports
Taxes levied on imports that have domestic equivalents.[7]

F71 Consumption taxes
A tax on sales of products which are generally applied to all or most products.
Example: *Sales tax, turnover tax (or multiple sales tax), value added tax.*

F72 Excise taxes
A tax imposed on selected types of commodities, usually of a luxurious or non-essential nature: This tax is levied separately from, and in addition to, the general sales taxes.
Example: Excise tax, tax on alcoholic consumption, cigarette tax.

F73 Taxes and charges for sensitive product categories
Charges that include emission charges, (sensitive) product taxes, and administrative charges: These latter charges are meant to recover the costs of administrative control systems.
Example: CO_2 *emission charge on motor vehicles.*

F79 Internal taxes and charges levied on imports n.e.s.

F8 Decreed Customs valuations
Value of goods determined by a decree for the purpose of imposition of customs duties and other charges: This practice is presented as a means to avoid fraud or to protect domestic industry. The decreed value de facto transforms an ad-valorem duty into a specific duty.
Example: the so-called "valeur mercuriale" in Francophone countries.

F9 Price control measures n.e.s.

G FINANCE MEASURES
Finance measures are intended to regulate the access to and cost of foreign exchange for imports and to define the terms of payment. They may increase import costs in the same manner as tariff measures.

G1 Advance payment requirement
Advance payment requirements related to the value of the import transaction and/or related import taxes: These payments are made at the time an application is lodged or when an import license is issued. They can consist of the following:

G11 Advance import deposit
A requirement that the importer should deposit a percentage of the value of the import transaction before receiving the goods: no interest is paid on the deposits.
Example: Payment of 50% of the transaction value is required three months before the expected arrival of the goods to the port of entry.

G12 Cash margin requirement

A requirement to deposit the total amount of the transaction value in a foreign currency, or a specified part of it, in a commercial bank, before the opening of a letter of credit.

Example: Deposit of 100% of the transaction value is required at the designated commercial bank.

G13 Advance payment of customs duties

A requirement to pay all or part of the customs duties in advance: no interest is paid on these advance payments.

Example: Payment of 100% of the estimated customs duty is required three months before the expected arrival of the goods to the port of entry.

G14 Refundable deposits for sensitive product categories

A requirement to pay a certain deposit which is refunded when the used product or its container is returned to a collection system.

Example: $100 deposit is required for each refrigerator, which will be refunded when brought in for recycling after use.

G19 Advance payment requirements n.e.s.

G2 Multiple exchange rates

Varying exchange rates for imports, depending on the product category: Usually, the official rate is reserved for essential commodities, while the other goods must be paid at commercial rates or occasionally by buying foreign exchange through auctions.[8]

Example: Only the payment for infant food and staple food imports may be made at the official exchange rate.

G3 Regulation on official foreign exchange allocation

G31 Prohibition of foreign exchange allocation

No official foreign exchange allocations available to pay for imports.

Example: Foreign exchange is not allocated for imports of luxury products such as motor vehicles, TV sets, jewelry, etc.,

G32 Bank authorization

A requirement to obtain a special import authorization from the central bank.

Example: For imports of motor vehicles, a central bank permit is required in addition to the import license.

G33 Authorization linked with non-official foreign exchange
License granted only if non-official foreign exchange is used for the import payment.

G331 External foreign exchange
License granted only for imports related to technical assistance projects and other sources of external foreign exchange.
Example: Imports of construction materials are allowed only if payments may be made through the foreign direct investment fund.

G332 Importers' own foreign exchange
License granted if the importer has his own foreign exchange held in an overseas bank.
Example: Imports of textile materials are authorized only if the importer could pay directly to the exporter with his own foreign exchange obtained through his export activity abroad.

G339 License linked with non-official foreign exchange, n.e.s.

G39 Regulation on official foreign exchange allocation, n.e.s.

G4 Regulations concerning terms of payment for imports
Regulations related to conditions of payment of imports and the obtaining and use of credit (foreign or domestic) to finance imports.
Example: No more than 50% of the transaction value can be paid in advance of the arrival of goods to the port of entry.

G9 Finance measures n.e.s.

H MEASURES AFFECTING COMPETITION
Measures to grant exclusive or special preferences or privileges to one or more limited group of economic operators.

H1 State trading enterprises, for importing; other selective import channels

H11 State trading enterprises, for importing
Enterprises (whether or not state-owned or state-controlled) with special rights and privileges not available to other entities,

which influence through their purchases and sales the level or direction of imports of particular products. (See also P2.)
Examples: A statutory marketing board with exclusive rights to control imports of certain grains, a canalizing agency with exclusive right to distribute petroleum, a sole importing agency, or importation reserved for specific importers regarding certain categories of goods.

H19 Other selective import channels n.e.s.

H2 Compulsory use of national services

H21 Compulsory national insurance
A requirement that imports must be insured by a national insurance company.

H22 Compulsory national transport
A requirement that imports must be carried by a national shipping company.

H29 Compulsory national service, n.e.s.

H9 Measures affecting competition n.e.s.

I TRADE-RELATED INVESTMENT MEASURES (TRIMS)[9,10]

I1 Local content measures
Requirements to purchase or use certain minimum levels or types of domestically produced or sourced products or restrictions on the purchase or use of imported products based on the volume or value of exports of local products.
Example: In the production of automobiles, locally produced components must account for at least 50% of the value of the components used.

I2 Trade balancing measures
Restrictions on the importation of products used in or related to local production, including in relation to the amount of local products exported; or limitations on access to foreign exchange used for such importation based on the foreign exchange inflows attributable to the enterprise in question.
Example: A company may import materials and other products only up to 80% of its export earnings of the previous year.

I9   Trade-related investment measures n.e.s.

Categories J to O below (marked with *) are included in the classification to collect information from the private sector through surveys and web-portals. Therefore, examples provided are type of "complaints" that may be expected to fall under the respective categories and sub-categories.

J DISTRIBUTION RESTRICTIONS*

Distribution of goods inside the importing country may be restricted. It may be controlled through additional license or certification requirement.[11]

J1 Geographical restriction

Restriction to limit the sales of goods to certain areas within the importing country.

Example: Imported beverages may only be sold in cities having facility to recycle the containers.

J2 Restriction on resellers

Restriction to limit the sales of imported products by designated retailers.

Example: Exporters of motor vehicles need to set up their own retail points as existing car dealers in the destination country belong exclusively to car producers in that country.

K RESTRICTION ON POST-SALES SERVICES*

Measures restricting producers of exported goods to provide post-sales service in the importing country.

Example: After-sales servicing on exported TV sets must be provided by local service company of the importing country.

L SUBSIDIES (EXCLUDING EXPORT SUBSIDIES UNDER P7)*

Financial contribution by a government or public body, or via government entrustment or direction of a private body (direct or potential direct transfer of funds: e.g., grant, loan, equity infusion, guarantee; government revenue foregone; provision of goods or services or purchase of goods; and payments to a funding mechanism), or income or price support, which confers a benefit and is specific (to an enterprise or industry or group thereof, or limited to a designated geographical region).

Example: The government provides producers of chemicals a one-time cash grant to replace antiquated production equipment.
Note: this category is to be further sub-divided after further study on the subject.

M GOVERNMENT PROCUREMENT RESTRICTIONS*
Measures controlling the purchase of goods by government agencies, generally by preferring national providers.
Example: Government office has a traditional supplier of its office equipment requirement, in spite of higher prices than similar foreign suppliers.

N INTELLECTUAL PROPERTY*
Measures related to intellectual property rights in trade: Intellectual property legislation covers patents, trademarks, industrial designs, layout designs of integrated circuits, copyright, geographical indications, and trade secrets.
Example: Clothing with unauthorized use of a trademark is sold at much lower price than the authentic products.

O RULES OF ORIGIN*
Rules of origin cover laws, regulations, and administrative determinations of general application applied by governments of importing countries to determine the country of origin of goods. Rules of origin are important in implementing such trade policy instruments as anti-dumping and countervailing duties, origin marking, and safeguard measures.
Example: Machinery products produced in a country are difficult to fulfill the rules of origin to qualify for the reduced tariff rate of the importing country, as the parts and materials originate in different countries.

P EXPORT-RELATED MEASURES
Export-related measures are measures applied by the government of the exporting country on exported goods.

P1 Export license, quota, prohibition, and other quantitative restrictions[12]
Restrictions to the quantity of goods exported to a specific country or countries by the government of the exporting country for reasons such as: shortage of goods in the domestic market, regulating domestic prices, avoiding antidumping measures, or for political reasons.[13]

P11 Export Prohibition
Prohibition of exports of certain products.
Example: Export of corn is prohibited because of shortage in domestic consumption.

P12 Export quotas
Quotas that limit value or volume of exports.
Example: Export quota of beef is established to guarantee adequate supply in the domestic market.

P13 Licensing or permit requirements to export
A requirement to obtain license or permit by the government of the exporting country to export products.
Example: Export of diamond ores are subject to licensing by the Ministry

P14 Export registration requirements
A requirement to register products before being exported (for monitoring purposes).
Example: Pharmaceutical products need to be registered before being exported.

P19 Export quantitative restrictions n.e.s.

P2 State trading enterprises, for exporting; other selective export channels

P21 State trading enterprises, for exporting
Enterprises (whether or not state-owned or state-controlled) with special rights and privileges not available to other entities, which influence through their purchases and sales the level or direction of exports of particular products. (See also H1.)
Example: An export monopoly board, to take advantage of terms of sale abroad; a marketing board, to promote for export on behalf of a large number of small farmers.

P29 Other selective export channels n.e.s.

P3 Export price control measures
Measures implemented to control the prices of exported products.
Example: Different prices for exports are applied from the same product sold in domestic market (dual pricing schemes).

P4 Measures on re-export

Measures applied by the government of the exporting country on exported goods which have originally been imported from abroad.

Example: Re-export of wines and spirits back to producing county is prohibited: the practice is common in cross-border trade to avoid imposition of domestic excise tax in the producing country.

P5 Export taxes and charges

Taxes collected on exported goods by the government of the exporting country: They can be set either on a specific or an ad valorem basis.

Example: Export duty on crude petroleum is levied for revenue purposes.

P6 Export technical measures

Export regulations referring to technical specification of products and conformity assessment systems thereof.

P61 Inspection requirement

Control over the quality or other characteristics of products for export.

Example: Exports of processed food products must be inspected for sanitary conditions.

P62 Certification required by the exporting country

Requirement by the exporting country to obtain sanitary, phytosanitary, or other certification before the goods are exported.

Example: Export of live animals must carry individual health certificate.

P69 Export technical measures n.e.s.

P7 Export subsidies

Financial contribution by a government or public body, or via government entrustment or direction of a private body (direct or potential direct transfer of funds: e.g., grant, loan, equity infusion, guarantee; government revenue foregone; provision of goods or services or purchase of goods; payments to a funding mechanism); or income or price support, which confers a benefit and is contingent in law or in fact upon export performance (whether solely or as one of several conditions), including measures illustrated in Annex I of the Agreement on Subsidies and Countervailing Measures and measures described in the Agreement on Agriculture.

Example: All manufacturers in Country A are exempt from income tax on their export profits.

P8 Export credits

P9 Export measures n.e.s.

Notes

1. Although quantitative restrictions are prohibited by the WTO Agreements, under the Agreement on Safeguards, safeguard measures in this form are permitted, subject to certain conditions.

2. Most quantity control measures are formally prohibited by the GATT 1994, but can be applied under specifically determined circumstances (e.g., Article XI of GATT 1994; Agreement on Safeguards: See E4, etc.).

3. Such arrangements are formally prohibited by the WTO Agreements.

4. These measures are prohibited by the WTO Agreements. Under the Agreements on Anti-dumping and on Subsidies and Countervailing Measures, however, measures in the form of price undertakings are permitted under certain conditions. See D13 and D23 for examples.

5. These measures are prohibited by the WTO Agreement on Agriculture, Article 4.

6. It should be noted that Article VIII of GATT states that fees and charges other than customs duties and internal taxes "shall be limited in amount to the approximate cost of services rendered and shall not represent an indirect protection to domestic products or a taxation of imports or exports for fiscal purposes."

7. Article III of the GATT Agreement allows internal taxes to be applied to imports; however, these taxes should not be higher than those applied to similar domestic products.

8. The use of multiple exchange rates is formally prohibited by the GATT 1994.

9. Subject to certain exceptions, the measures listed in I1-I3 are inconsistent with the TRIMs Agreement (respectively, the obligations of national treatment under Article III and general elimination of QRs under Article XI of GATT 1994). See Illustrative List annexed to the TRIMs Agreement.

10. Trade-related investment measures in the form of export restrictions are included in category P1.

11. These restrictions are closely related with regulations of distribution services.

12. Trade-related investment measures in the form of export restrictions are included in this category.

13. All of these measures are formally prohibited by the GATT 1994, but may be applied under specific situations identified in Article XI of GATT 1994.

Request Form for NTM Review

This questionnaire illustrates some of the important information a reviewer of a non-tariff measure (NTM) should collect before initiating a full regulatory review at the request of an applicant, be it a firm, a business association, or a nongovernmental organization (NGO). This review will determine whether a full review is justified or unjustified and not worth dedicating scarce human and financial resources. The reviewer should be convinced that the NTM is doing real harm; the burden of proof initially lies with the applicants.

Information to be Provided by the Applicant

1. The identity of the applicant (name, address, and telephone number of the applicant).
   - If the application is made on behalf of the domestic industry, it shall identify the industry on behalf of which the application is made by a list of all known domestic producers of the like product (or associations of domestic producers), total employment, number of firms, share of total exports and GDP.
   - If the applicant is a firm, it shall provide information on its size (including total sales, employment, and so on).

- If the applicant is a citizen, NGO, or other representative of civil society, it shall provide information on the group it represents (including number of people, geographical location, income level).

2. A description of the measure or issue to be reviewed (for example, law, procedure, or delay/cost) and the responsible agency or ministry.
3. A description of the product(s)/service(s) affected (for example, HS number).
4. A quantitative and qualitative description of the negative impact of the above measure in terms of:
   - cost of production
   - business opportunities on the export market
   - quality of the goods and services produced
   - productivity
   - competition
   - administrative procedures
   - safety
   - health

5. Information and summary results of previous initiatives to solve the problem with the government and/or among the group (private sector or civil society).
6. A description of a suggested solution to the problem if available.

Questionnaire for the Review of Existing NTMs

The following questionnaire will help policy makers and analysts conduct a regulatory review of non-tariff measures (NTMs) following some guiding principles along three dimensions in the areas of design of the regulation and its enforcement/compliance:

1. Governance: Questions aim at checking whether measures are transparent (for example, simplicity of the legal text and availability of the information to traders) and whether there are issues with their implementation and enforcement;
2. Legal consistency: Questions aim at checking whether the measures are consistent with the country's World Trade Organization (WTO) obligation (in particular SPS [sanitary and phytosanitary] and TBT [technical barriers to trade] agreements), with the country's treaties, and with other domestic pieces of legislation; and
3. Performance: These questions aim at assessing the coherence of the measure design, including across regulations (for example, between measures affecting domestic production and those affecting import) and along the value chain; adequacy of the measure to the problem (proportionality, targeting); and overall performance in alleviating the motivating market failure.

Assessment Guidelines

These guidelines are designed to help the analyst get useful information and quantification of the issues from the private sector and from national authorities. Responses can be consolidated in the same document. Short explanations are provided for those questions that are not self-explanatory.

The Measure's ID Card

1. *Please give (or append) the text of the measure. When was it adopted?*
2. *What is the legal nature of the measure (law, presidential or ministerial decree, and so on)?*
   Please identify the NTM category of the measure (see appendix A for a standard classification of NTMs).
3. *What is the level (or levels) of government for this measure (central, sub-central, municipal). What was the issuing agency?*
4. *What are the agency or agencies in charge of enforcement?*
5. *Please specify as precisely as possible what product or category of products is concerned, using the HS system. Is this product or product category predominantly a final (consumer) or intermediate/primary product?*

WTO Consistency

6. *Is the measure accessible to users? How? Is it available online? If yes, please provide web address.*
7. *Is the language of the measure comprehensible to non-specialists? Is it available in foreign languages for foreign exporters? (for example, in WTO official languages—English, Spanish, or French)*
8. *Is there an international legal basis for the regulation? If yes, what treaty/agreement and, if applicable, what article?*
9. *Was the measure notified to the WTO? If yes, under what agreement? If no, what was the reason for not notifying it?*
10. *If the regulation was meant to protect human health or the environment, was it science-based? Please provide a source for the scientific evidence used (laboratory tests, scientific articles, or expert opinion).*

Assessing the Measure's Benefits

11. *Please define clearly the problem that the measure was meant to address (human health, product compatibility, etc.)*
    This question is meant to help the analyst to determine to what extent the measure addresses a "market failure." It is key to establishing justification of the measure.

12. *How important is the primary risk being addressed by the measure? Can it be somehow quantified?*
    This is one of the most important issues. Responses here should determine whether the review ought to bring in outside expertise—for example, environmental or health experts from the local university.

13. *Please explain practically how the regulation addresses the problem, that is, by what mechanism the measure will have the intended effect.*
    Here the ministry in charge should be as clear and specific as possible.

14. *Does the problem still exist?*
    The issue here is whether technology or other market changes have made the regulation obsolete. For instance, it may address a health hazard that does not exist anymore or was demonstrated by scientists to be nonexistent.

15. *All in all, how successful has the measure been at achieving its objective? What are the main constraints to its effectiveness?*
    The issue here is whether there are faults in the regulation's design that make it ineffective. Loopholes are specifically dealt with in Question 34.

16. *Can private operators somehow take care of the problem through cooperation, voluntary labeling, or other mechanisms?*
    This question gives an opportunity to producers to explain how they could voluntarily alleviate the problem of concern to the government. For instance, this can include voluntary labeling, environmental certification, "corporate social responsibility" initiatives, traceability, or other efforts.

17. *Is the problem arising from production or use/consumption?*
    The issue here is whether there is any health hazard related to consumption of the product, in which case the measure should either affect the product's design to ensure it is safe, or restrict its sale; alternatively, whether there is any health hazard with production (say, because its production generates polluting effluents or creates an occupational hazard to the health of workers), in which case the measure should take the form of a production standard, not an NTM.

18. *Who are the main beneficiaries of the measure? Does the measure have any side benefits?*

    Here the response should indicate any sector of activity, occupation, or category of residents primarily benefiting from the measure. "Side benefit" of a product standard, for example, might include technological upgrading.

Assessing the Regulation's Costs through Design

19. *Did the measure raise the price of imported products? If yes, which ones and by how much? Please provide estimates.*

    This is one of the key questions, thus a response as precise and quantitative as possible should be sought from affected producers/importers. By how much, in percentage, has the import price risen as a result of the measure? What country would provide a good comparison to estimate the price rise induced by the measure?

20. *Which industries/firms were most affected by the measure? What was the effect on their employment, production, and exports? What is the share of affected industries in (a) trade and (b) employment?*

    Again, quantitative estimates should be sought out, not just for the respondent's firm, but if possible for the whole industry.

21. *Were compensatory/adjustment assistance measures put in place for those negatively affected by the measure?*

    These may include, for example, indirect subsidies of any form or the provision of government services at less than full-recovery costs.

22. *Did the measure restrict import volumes? If yes, please provide tentative estimates.*

    Respondents may have difficulty answering this question, which can be addressed by econometric/simulation methods outside of the questionnaire.

23. *Did the measure purposely or incidentally affect the import mix (in terms of origin, quality, or other) or reduce the variety of goods sold on the domestic market?*

    For instance, a quota may induce foreign producers to specialize in the upper segment of the market in order to maximize their profit margins on each unit sold. A technical regulation may also shift the spectrum of imported products toward higher quality.

24. *Is the regulated product domestically produced? Did the measure lead to an increase/decrease in domestic production/investment?*

    The response to this question may overlap somewhat with that of questions 18 and 20—its objective is to ascertain whether an import restriction benefits domestic producers.

25. *Did the measure lead to a change in competition among importers or producers?*
Here the objective is to ascertain whether the measure benefited some producers at the expense of others. For instance, a technical regulation imposing the use of high-price intermediates may be difficult to meet for small-scale producers. It is important for the analyst to understand, through responses to this and other questions, whether producers voicing their views about a measure are representative of the whole industry or only a segment of it.

26. *Are vulnerable groups affected (small-scale enterprises, particular sub-groups of population like indigenous peoples)?*

27. *What are the gender effects, if any?*
Some measures may have unintended consequences on the ability of women to do business. For instance, when information on regulations is not available through formal channels, it may be available only to informal, male-dominated networks.

Assessing the Regulation's Costs for Implementation/Enforcement

28. *What is legally required of traders (importers or exporters) to be in compliance with the measure?*
Responses to this question should include all procedures and paperwork. Any discrepancy in answers between government officials and private operators should be carefully discussed.

29. *How is compliance with the measure verified? Please explain the entire procedure, including each step. Is there risk management at the border?*
One of the key issues here is whether there is "risk profiling" or, instead, whether all shipments are systematically inspected.

30. *How long, on average, does it take to be granted a permit? Is there a transparent, publicly available timeline?*

31. *Are permits permanent or must they be renewed periodically? If renewal is necessary, on what basis?*
Here it is important to distinguish between certification permits, which establish the status of the importer, and import permits, which verify compliance with any measure such as quantity limits or technical regulations.

32. *How frequently are permits or necessary documentation denied or delayed? Provide the most frequent reasons.*
Here it may be useful to have practical examples of permits being denied without valid reason, and such examples may subsequently be discussed with enforcing agencies in the government.

33. *Do traders need to pay fees to be in compliance? Please specify nature of fees and amount, if applicable.*
Here it would be useful to get a feel for the size of the fees relative to the value of the shipment, in percentage.

34. *Are there loopholes in enforcement? Please explain.*
Loopholes to be discussed here include both those due to faulty design and those due to discriminatory administration—for instance, ad hoc exemptions granted to politically connected operators.

35. *Is the regulation generating revenue to the government or is it mobilizing resources? Please explain and if possible provide estimates of revenues or costs.*

How the Measure Was Adopted

36. *Was there a consultation process? Was the consultation process standard or ad hoc? If standard, please specify what guidelines were followed. Were some stakeholders proactively sought (consumers, nongovernmental organizations, and so on)?*

37. *If there was a consultation process, what were the main issues raised by stakeholders? Were there strong views one way or another?*

38. *What alternative measures were considered and discarded? Please provide a short explanation for the choices made.*

39. *Does the measure have a sunset clause? Has the measure been reviewed? If yes, by whom and what was the result of the review?*

Price Gap and Welfare

Derivation of the Price-Gap Formula

This appendix details the derivation of the price-gap formula (see chapters 2 and 5) under two assumptions: (1) the simplest case, where there are no systematic differences in the cost of living between the home country and the country chosen as a comparator, and (2) the more complicated case, where there are systematic differences. The first case is not realistic and is reviewed only in order to start with a simple formula, so as to build realism (and complication) step by step.

Case 1: No Systematic Cost-of-Living Difference

Let P_i^* be the international price of product i, which is assumed as fixed in international markets. Later on, we will discuss in what sense this assumption is not realistic and how to amend it to something more realistic. Also, let t_i^H and t_i^C be the ad-valorem tariffs applied to product i in the home (H) and comparator (C) countries, respectively. Let P_i^H be the domestic price of product i on the home market and P_i^C its domestic price in the comparator country. Assume that a non-tariff measure (NTM) is imposed by the home country on widgets, for which we will omit the index i, and let a be the ad-valorem equivalent (AVE) of that NTM, in fractional form (that is, the AVE in percent form is 100 times a).

No NTM is imposed on widgets in the comparator country, which is why we chose it. We do not know a but will determine it using information that is available, which is essentially

- the domestic price of widgets and other products in the home and comparator markets and
- tariff rates applies to widgets and other products in the home and comparator markets.

Formally, the home price of widgets is determined by

$$p^H = p^*(1+t^H)(1+a) \tag{1}$$

where a is unknown, and its price in the comparator market by

$$p^C = p^*(1+t^C) \tag{2}$$

In (1) and (2), everything is observed except a. Therefore, we can take the ratio of the two and obtain

$$\frac{p^H}{p^C} = \frac{p^*(1+t^H)(1+a)}{p^*(1+t^C)} \tag{3}$$

On the left-hand side (LHS) is the ratio of domestic prices observed in the home and comparator markets, which is the main piece of evidence we use in the price-gap calculation. If the home price of widgets is three times their price in the comparator market, the ratio of the LHS is 3. On the right-hand side is an expression involving the common international price, p^*, which can be eliminated, and tariffs. We can invert this expression to isolate $(1 + a)$, obtaining:

$$\frac{p^H/(1+t^H)}{p^C/(1+t^C)} = 1+a \tag{4}$$

or

$$a = \frac{p^H/(1+t^H)}{p^C/(1+t^C)} - 1. \tag{5}$$

That is, the AVE of the NTM on widgets is calculated as the ratio of the home and comparator prices of widgets "purged" of the effect of tariffs.

The reason for taking tariffs into account is as follows. Suppose that observed domestic prices in the home and comparator countries, converted into US dollars at the current exchange rate, are \$16.2 and \$12.0, respectively, and tariffs are 20 percent and 5 percent respectively. Without tariff adjustment, the estimated AVE would be

$$a_{\text{unadjusted}} = \frac{16.2}{12.0} - 1 = 0.35$$

or 35.0 percent, suggesting that the NTM imposed on widgets raises their home price by 35.0 percent. However the tariff-adjusted AVE is

$$a_{\text{tariff-adjusted}} = \frac{16.2/(1+20/100)}{12/(1+5/100)} - 1 = \frac{16.2/1.2}{12/1.05} - 1 = 0.1813$$

or 18.13 percent. That is, almost half of the difference in the price of widgets between the home and comparator markets is accounted for by the difference in tariff rates. Attributing the whole price difference to the NTM would be flat wrong.

Case 2: Systematic Cost-of-Living Difference

Now suppose that there are unobserved or hard-to-measure factors that raise the cost of living (COL) in the home country to a level that is systematically higher than in the comparator country. These factors can include transportation costs, landlockedness, port inefficiency, and so on—as long as they are not themselves due to NTMs. Let λ be the common price-raising factor affecting all products. Then (1) becomes

$$p^H = p^*(1+\lambda)(1+t^H)(1+a) \tag{6}$$

whereas (2) is unchanged. Combining (6) and (2) as we did in (5), we have

$$a = \frac{p^H / \left[(1+t^H)(1+\lambda) \right]}{p^C / (1+t^C)} - 1. \tag{7}$$

So now we have two unknowns to determine: α and λ. For that, we need some additional information. That information will be obtained by looking at price differences for other products, preferably not subject to any cost-raising NTMs (finding such products is part of the difficulty of this exercise). Suppose we have found 30 such products, and let $\bar{p}^H$ and

$\bar{p}^C$ be their average prices on the home and comparator markets, respectively. We can write

$$\bar{p}^H = \bar{p}^* (1+\lambda)(1+\bar{t}^H)$$
$$\bar{p}^C = \bar{p}^* (1+\lambda)(1+\bar{t}^C)v,$$

so, after manipulation,

$$\lambda = \frac{\bar{p}^H / (1+\bar{t}^H)}{\bar{p}^C / (1+\bar{t}^C)} - 1. \tag{8}$$

Thus, we now calculate the price gap in two steps:

Step 1. Calculate the COL adjustment λ factor using (8).
Step 2. Calculate the price gap using domestic prices, tariffs, and the estimate of λ obtained from step 1.

In the example above, a COL adjustment of 18 percent would be enough to wipe out completely the estimated AVE of the NTM, meaning that the initial price difference of 35 percent on widgets would be explained roughly in half by tariffs and in half by systematic COL differences.

An Econometric Approach

The price-gap method can be likened to an econometric approach known as "difference in differences" (DID), and the analogy may help readers who are familiar with econometrics to understand how it works. Assume that we have price data for a sample of products, defined at the HS6 level of the Harmonized system's nomenclature, and a sample of countries (more than two, unlike before). Some of those products are covered by the NTM in some but not all of the countries, but there are product-country combinations without *any* price-raising NTM.

The DID regression estimates the correlation between prices (the dependent variable, in log form) with explanatory variables including tariffs and "dummy" (binary zero/one) variables marking the presence of NTMs. Let k be a product, i a country, and n a type of NTMs (say, $n = A$ means an SPS, $n = B$ a TBT, and so on).

Let

$$I_{ikn} = \begin{cases} 1 & \text{if NTM } n \text{ is imposed by country } i \text{ on product } k \\ 0 & \text{otherwise.} \end{cases}$$

The DID regression equation has the form

$$\ln p_i = \alpha \ln (1+t_i) + \sum_{n=A,\ldots} \beta_n I_{ikn} + \delta_i + \delta_k + u_{ik} \qquad (9)$$

where u_i is an error term. "Fixed effects" δ_i and δ_k control respectively for systematic cost-of-living differences across countries and for the fact that we are literally comparing apples and oranges in the regression since we are pooling over products. If the sample is declared as a panel with products as the panel's "individuals", the econometrics software will transform the price data by subtracting the mean sample price of each product, in effect converting prices into price gaps. Using hats to denote econometric estimates, the estimated AVE of NTM n across countries and products is

$$AVE_n = e^{\hat{\beta}_n} - 1. \qquad (10)$$

Derivation of the Welfare Formula

This appendix section details the derivation of the formula mapping price changes into welfare changes, under the assumption that the utility function is such that there is an equivalence between welfare changes and monetary income changes that is not affected by policy changes (this is true, for instance, when the utility function is quasi-linear).

When analyzing preferential tariff reductions, much of the complication in welfare calculations comes from the differential treatment of preferential vs. non-preferential partners, which induces trade-diversion effects in addition to trade-creation ones. By contrast, most NTMs—though not all—are applied on an MFN (most favored nation) basis, so there are no trade-diversion issues. The most important exceptions are quotas and tariff-quotas applied as part of preferential agreements, for example, in the context of agricultural products in EU preferences, but those tend to get phased out. Accordingly, in what follows, we will treat only the case of NTMs applied on an MFN basis.

Let $\Delta p < 0$ be the change in the domestic price generated by the elimination of an NTM, and let $\Delta C > 0$ be the corresponding increase in domestic consumption of the product in question. The effect of eliminating the NTM on consumer surplus is the sum of the rectangular and triangular areas (the total area $ABCD$ in figure 2.2 in chapter 2). That is, using the formula for the area of a right-angle triangle as an approximation to any non-linear demand curve:

$$\Delta W = C_0 \underbrace{(-\Delta p)}_{+} + \frac{1}{2} \underbrace{(-\Delta p)}_{+} \Delta C \qquad (11)$$

We know that the elasticity of demand, in algebraic form, is

$$\varepsilon = \frac{p_0}{C_0}\frac{\Delta C}{\Delta p} < 0 \tag{12}$$

So the change in consumption, ΔC, can be expressed in terms of the elasticity of demand and the change in the price, Δp.

$$\Delta C = C_0 \varepsilon \frac{\Delta p}{p_0} \tag{13}$$

Substituting (13) into (11) gives

$$
\begin{aligned}
\Delta W &= C_0\left(-\Delta p\right) + \frac{1}{2} C_0 \varepsilon \Delta p \left(\frac{-\Delta p}{p_0}\right) \\
&= p_0 C_0 \left(\frac{-\Delta p}{p_0}\right) - \frac{1}{2} p_0 C_0 \varepsilon \left(\frac{\Delta p}{p_0}\right)^2 \\
&= E_0 a - \frac{1}{2} E_0 \varepsilon a^2 \\
&= E_0 a\left(1 - \frac{\varepsilon a}{2}\right)
\end{aligned}
\tag{14}
$$

which is the formula in the text. Note that, in this formula, all "real" quantities (which are not observed) have been replaced by monetary ones (which are observed), by multiplying C_0 by p_0.

The Cost of Irreversible Decisions

This appendix section shows how to handle irreversible decisions and low-probability risks of large losses, highlighting the sensitivity of calculations to the data.

Case 1: Real Options and Irreversible Decisions

Traditional cost-benefit analysis consists of replacing uncertain magnitudes by the expected value and then comparing them. However, when some options are irreversible, this can be gravely misleading, as was shown by Henry (1974). His celebrated article was motivated by a demand from the French ministries of equipment and transport to evaluate, using cost-benefit analysis, a decision to cut through the forest of Rambouillet to build a highway around Paris. Henry showed that, with the decision to destroy a forest being irreversible, the analysis could not be correctly reduced to a comparison of expected costs and benefits. To see why, consider the following example.

Suppose that a domestic firm is losing money, and that the government is weighing the option to support it with some measure whose cost to society just matches its benefit to the firm, which means that it "nets out" in the calculation of social welfare. There are two periods, "today" (the first or current period, marked by the subscript 0) and "tomorrow" (the second period, market by the subscript 1). Profits and losses incurred tomorrow are discounted at rate r, and $\delta = 1/(1 + r)$ is the discount factor. The firm's current profit is $\pi 0$. In the second period, its profit is a random variable $\tilde{\pi}$ with distribution

$$\tilde{\pi} = \begin{cases} \pi^+ & \text{with prob. } p \\ \pi^- & \text{with prob. } 1-p \end{cases}$$

with $\pi^- < 0$ and $\pi^+ < 0$.

Assume that

A1. $\pi_0 < 0$

A2. $p\pi^+ + (1-p)\pi^- < 0$

A3. $\pi_0 + \delta p\pi^+ > 0$

Assumption A1 means that the firm's current profit is negative, and A2 means that its expected profit over the two-period horizon is also negative. Without government support, the firm closes down. But why should the government support it? Suppose that the government behaves like a rational shareholder. If it lets the firm close down, the payoff is zero with certainty. If it lends support, the firm will remain in business but, by A2, face more expected losses in the second period. A simple cost-benefit analysis suggests that the government should terminate support to the firm at once.

This reasoning is wrong. In period 2, if the "state of nature" is unfavorable ($\tilde{\pi} = \pi^-$) the government will let the firm close down and lose nothing. If it is favorable, then it will internalize the firm's profit ($\tilde{\pi} = \pi^+ > 0$). Thus, if the government supports the firm today, its expected payoff for the two periods is

$$\pi_{\text{support}} = \pi_0 + \delta p\pi^+ \tag{15}$$

Whereas if it does not, its payoff is

$$\pi_{\text{let down}} = 0 \tag{16}$$

By A3, the government is better off supporting the firm. The reason is that in doing so it keeps the option of closing it down tomorrow, if the state of nature turns out to be bad, but enjoying positive profits if it is good. By closing down the firm today, it forecloses the possibility of enjoying the positive profits tomorrow.

Thus, keeping the support today is like holding an option on a stock. That option has a value that can be calculated using option-pricing techniques (see Dixit and Pindyck 1994 for technical details). There are many applications of this principle, for instance, to environmental decisions. The next section of this appendix considers a slight variant where a decision tree reaches a terminal node when a policy decision triggers a certain event.

Case 2: An Irreversible Risk

Consider the following situation. A sanitary and phytosanitary (SPS) regulation prohibits the import of a plant that may carry an invasive micro-organism. If the regulation was relaxed (a binary decision), there would be an annual probability of a disease outbreak equal to p, and the monetary cost of the outbreak, which would be irreversible, would be L. This cost includes the present value, in monetary terms, of all damages inflicted to the economy and the environment. For instance, if the industry was wiped out by the outbreak, L would include the present value of all future lost production. The prohibition's annual cost to domestic producers, who would otherwise use the plant as an input, is C. Let V_I be the value to the government of sticking to the regulation, and V_O the value of eliminating it. Also let $\delta = 1/(1 + r)$ be the discount factor. We have

$$V_I = -C + \delta \max\{V_I; V_O\}$$
$$V_O = -pL + (1-p)\delta \max\{V_I; V_O\} \qquad (17)$$

Suppose that $V_O < V_1$. Then

$$V_I = -C + \delta V = -C/(1-\delta)$$
$$V_O = -pL + (1-p)\delta V_I$$

$$= -pL - (1-p)\frac{\delta}{1-\delta}C \qquad (18)$$

So we must have

$$-pL-(1-p)\frac{\delta}{1-\delta}C<-\frac{C}{1-\delta} \qquad (19)$$

or, after rearrangement,

$$\frac{C}{1-\delta}<\frac{pL}{1-\delta(1-p)}. \qquad (20)$$

The LHS is the present discounted value of an infinite stream of costs, C, what the economy would suffer if the regulation was maintained forever. The RHS is the cost of facing, year after year, the probability of an outbreak costing L, which is what the economy would face if the regulation was eliminated. If, after substituting estimated values for p, C, and L, the three key parameters, the inequality is as shown in (20), the regulation should be maintained. If it is reversed, the regulation should be eliminated.

How should the parameters p, C, and L be estimated? Rough estimates of C and L should be obtained from producers and government authorities. As for p, it is the probability that, absent the prohibition, an infected plant would be imported. Suppose that N plants are imported each year and n are tested for the disease by sanitary authorities at the border, and if a single plant tests positive, the whole shipment is destroyed. Assume for simplicity that all imports arrive in one shipment of N plants, n of which will be tested. The probability of importing at least one infected plant and having none testing positive is the product of two independent probabilities: (1) the probability of none testing positive in the sample tested, and (2) the probability of at least one being infected in the sample not tested.

Suppose that the ex-ante probability of any given plant being infected is q. Let us call the first event (nondetection) ND. Its probability is that of having exactly zero "success" (a success is a plant testing positive) in n trials given a probability of "success" (infection) equal to q. This probability is given by the binomial formula, with $k = 0$:

$$\Pr(ND)=\binom{n}{k}q^k(1-q)^{n-k} \qquad (21)$$

This boils down to $(1-q)^n$. By the same reasoning, the second probability is one minus the probability of having no infection in the nontested part of the shipment, that is, $1-(1-q)^{N-n}$. Thus,

$$p=\left[1-(1-q)^{N-n}\right](1-q)^n. \qquad (22)$$

A note of caution must be stated. How sensitive are the calculations to assumptions? The answer is, very sensitive, and in ways which may sound surprising. To see this, consider the following example.

Suppose that annual export sales are $4.4 million. Assume, as a first approximation, that this is all value-added (as if the production was organic agriculture), and that the regulation cuts 10 percent from this total. Thus, the annual loss in value added is $440,000. This is C. Assume that an outbreak would cost the industry $23 million. Furthermore, assume that the industry imports 30,000 plants each year and that the quarantine service tests 2 percent of them. Finally, let the discount rate be 7 percent.

The present discounted value of the regulation's cost, $C/(1 - \delta)$, is $6.7 million. Suppose first that the probability of infection of any given plant is 1/100,000. Then the expected cost of lifting the regulation is $19 million. That is, even without counting the environmental damage, the damage the industry would inflict on itself by taking the risk of an infection would far outweigh the possible benefit. By contrast, suppose now that the probability of infection of any given plant is 1/20. Then the expected cost of lifting the regulation is zero. This may seem very odd. The reason is that, with a probability of infection of 1/100,000, sampling at a 2 percent rate has a very low probability of catching an infected plant (less than 1 percent), while importing 30,000 of them carries a substantial risk (25 percent). By contrast, with a probability of 1/20, sampling at 2 percent is very efficient: the probability of catching an infected plant is almost 100 percent. Thus, even though the probability of infection is also very high (even closer to 100 percent), the testing is sufficiently reliable to rule out undetected infection. In fact, the testing acts like a prohibition, because, with such a high probability of infection, all shipments test positive and are destroyed.

References

Dixit, Avinash, and R. Pyndick. 1994. *Investment Under Uncertainty*. Princeton, NJ: Princeton University Press.

Henry, Claude. 1974. "Investment Decisions Under Uncertainty: The 'Irreversibility Effect.'" *American Economic Review* 64 (6): 1006–12.

www.ingramcontent.com/pod-product-compliance
Lightning Source LLC
Chambersburg PA
CBHW061734270326
41928CB00011B/2226